P9-DYZ-412

THERE'S MUSIC IN CHILDREN

THERE'S MUSIC IN CHILDREN

Revised and Enlarged Edition

EMMA DICKSON SHEEHY

NEW YORK: HENRY HOLT AND COMPANY

27843-0112

August, 1957

Library of Congress Catalog Card Number 52-10282

PRINTED IN THE UNITED STATES OF AMERICA

PREFACE TO REVISED EDITION

LOVE FOR MUSIC is as natural in little children as their love for play. It is this truth, which so often escapes people, that is the core of this book, and the book is the outgrowth of long experience as a classroom teacher with young children, with teachers of children, and with parents. Unfortunately, many grownups have had unhappy experiences with music when they were young, which have made them feel not only uncomfortable with it but also inadequate in helping children. It is skill in understanding children, however, and not skill in music techniques that will bring the greatest rewards in fostering a child's love for music. It is an inescapable, and a very happy, fact that there is music in everybody—in varying degrees, of course—but the potentialities are there.

The kind of environment that we provide both in the home and school is the most important single factor in determining children's attitude toward music, and the kind of attitude children have toward music is of tremendous importance in their learning. In this book I have tried to explore with the reader some of the many ways in which children learn about music and how they use it, and I have set down a few concrete suggestions for guiding these beginning learnings. *There is no system or method as such*—this is most important to remember—but there are ways of helping all of us become more keenly aware of the beginnings of music in children, the importance of our feelings about these, and the role of guidance. In Chapters 7 and 8 I have discussed a few ways in which grownups can help themselves identify with the "materials" of music so as to better understand children's growth. These suggestions have developed through working together with many students (experienced classroom teachers) at Teachers College, in conference groups with teachers in many sections of the United States, and with parent groups, and represent only a few of the ways possible for adults to rediscover their own musical selves and grow in confidence. This book is dedicated to the proposition that music is a part of life, that there is music in *children and grownups,* and that we can always begin where we are and discover more about its pleasures.

Teachers College, Columbia University, 1952 E. D. S.

To Judy and Jonathan

CONTENTS

1

CHILDREN AND SOUND

SOUND is in the air; wherever we are, we are in the midst of it. Even if we wished, we could not escape the infinite variety of sounds in the world around us. Though some people are immune to them, we must all, if we wish to retain our sanity, develop protection against many environmental sounds. They may soothe or annoy; we may welcome them or run away from them. But we may as well accept the fact that many of them are inescapable.

Children take to sounds and sound-making as ducks to water. They not only accept them, but they also have a knack of adding to them until the other members of the family cannot endure the din. Then, even though they are admonished and sent out of earshot, this passion of theirs is somehow never completely satisfied. Here is one "talent" of youth that will not be kept down. Sometimes we grown-ups like it too, especially when *we* are the sound-makers. Whooping it up, now and then, serves to let off steam at any age.

Political campaigns would fall flat without noise. Try to imagine a baseball or football game in a soundproof stadium! Returning heroes are greeted with wild outbursts. The joys of the Old Year and the hopes for the New reach their peak of excitement on New Year's Eve. Even the quietest person can seldom resist noise-making at this time.

No, the interest in sound and sound-making does not belong exclusively to the time of childhood. "Sugar is not so sweet to the palate as sound to the healthy ear," quotes Emerson from an unpublished manuscript by Thoreau. In an essay on the subject he refers a number of times to Thoreau's sensitivity to sound, to the music in the humming of the telegraph wires, and the "z-ing" of the locust. Thoreau's "eye was open to beauty, his ear to music."

Why then are we so deaf to the instinctive early interest in sound possessed by every normal human being? Why the broken continuity between it and the study of music? Music is sounds put together. To be sure, the way in which they are put together makes all the difference in the kind of music it is. But—and this is certain—there is no one right way, no one wrong way. Nor is there any one way of teaching music to children. But if we can, in some way or another, hitch this tremendous interest in sounds and in sound-making to music, *and start with the child,* we shall have gone a long way toward encouraging a natural love for music.

Primitive man made music, not by playing notes but by experimenting and listening. Children learn to talk by experimenting and listening. And they can learn to make music by experimenting and listening. Unless we stop them!

It is for us to seize the children's enthusiasm at the floodtide. They will probably not turn out to be great musicians, but they will have a good time and they will most surely develop a genuine love for music. They will learn a surprising amount about it, too. And, if we do happen to have a budding genius in our child, what better way of cultivating his creative powers than to develop from the start the music he has within him?

CHILDREN USE THEIR VOICES IN EXPERIMENTING WITH SOUND

Is there anything that brings quite so much delight as the first babbling of the tiny baby? Unintelligible though it is, it tells us in no uncertain terms that this little bit of humanity is at peace with his world. He has discovered something he can do that gives him a thrill. Then it isn't long before he tumbles into the delights of sounding easy syllables and repeating them endlessly. Gradually some of these sounds, like "ma-ma" and "da-da," take on meaning; at least, we adults are always eager to attach meaning to them. But, meaning or no meaning, Junior happily pursues his "babbling career."

One of the ways we foster this early interest in sounds is through Mother Goose and other nursery rhymes. Children revel in the clash and repetition of words. "Higgledy, piggledy," "Diddle, diddle, dumpling," "Hickory, dickory, dock"—with their meaningless sounds and infectious rhythms—give endless satisfaction.

Children open their mouths and sounds come out. Accidentally they hit upon some that have particular appeal. Over and over, they repeat these to the point of self-intoxication. Perhaps this interest reaches its peak around the age of five or six. It is hard to say, for it is generally not encouraged by the family; it is even discouraged, since grownups can usually see no earthly reason why this nonsensical prattle should send their youngsters into peals of uncontrolled hilarity. Too often they regard it only as a child's weapon for persecuting his elders.

But it is not only children who revel in this play with words and sounds. There are, for example, certain poets who became famous because of their veritable genius in word sounds and word invention. The verse of Edward Lear is frankly nonsense and does not pretend to be anything else—and therein lies its charm. In order really to enjoy it, one must make it a part of oneself, and be able to roll it out on an instant's notice. Children are never-ceasing in their demands on someone who has a store of Edward Lear verses. They may sing along with the poetry, or be content merely to listen.

Many a bit of children's dead-end chatter can be turned into a constructive interest in what other people have done with words.

> There was an old person of Ware,
> Who rode on the back of a bear;
> When they said, "Does it trot?"
> He said, "Certainly, not!
> It's a Moppsikon Floppsikon bear!"[1]

Mopp-si-kon, Flopp-si-kon—how children like to lean on these words, play with them, invent more of their own, and go jingling on their way!

Laura E. Richards has delighted several generations of children and adults with her rhymes. She plays with words as a child does, and her nonsensical humor sends youngsters into gales of laughter. What is funnier than the mixing up of "elephant" and "telephone" to *telephant* and *elephone?* And is anyone's education complete without skinny "Mrs. Snipkin" and fat "Mrs. Wobblechin"?[2]

Every home, every school, should possess copies of Edward Lear and Laura E. Richards. But reading to the child from

[1] Edward Lear. *The Complete Nonsense Book*. Dutton.

[2] Laura E. Richards. *Tirra Lirra: Rhymes Old and New.* Little, Brown.

them is only a substitute for the ability to draw upon them at will wherever one is. We cannot, of course, have at the tip of our tongue all we could wish, but the more quickly we can recite or sing these bits, the more vital will be the experiences we can give to children. For, with young as with old, seizing the mood is the secret of interest and enthusiasm, and if we have to go to a book or a piano for everything we sing, we miss the spontaneous joy that comes to those who sing as they work or play, whether it be poetry or music.

Poetry *is* music. Not long ago Bobby's mother told us that he disliked poetry very much. She had been accustomed to reading it to him at bedtime, and he resisted it so much that she finally stopped. Then she said: "Bobby has been coming home from school recently, bubbling over with snatches of Lear, Richards, Milne, and Carroll—so I told him *that* was poetry, too." "It is not!" he shouted; "I don't *like* poetry!"

"Will you please," pleaded Bobby's mother, who has a genuine love for literature, "will you please tell Bobby that what he is enjoying so much *is* poetry?" "Not on your life," we said; "not now, at any rate, for we care not what he thinks it is. Names are 'noise and smoke.'" We knew our young Bobby too well to risk spoiling his fun by telling him something he did not want to hear.

The mature adult enjoys poetry for its construction, its meaning, its figures of speech, as well as for its sound and its rhythm. Little children judge poetry and song with their feelings, not with their intellects. This does not mean that we should expose them only to so-called children's poetry. If we go back in our own memories, we may be surprised at what we find. One recalls the magic-sounding words in Coleridge's *Kubla Khan;* another, Noyes's *The Highwayman* and its impelling rhythm; another, some special Psalm of David; and still another, Shelley's *The Cloud*. No doubt these had little meaning for us at the time, but they are remembered for their sounds, their rhythms, and their associations.

Children's lives are made rich with these experiences if those with whom they live have a genuine love and appreciation for the music of poetry. Play with them as they play with words, give them stories and verse to stimulate their imaginations, and, especially, let them enjoy it all in their own way. The fun of living it with father and mother, with teacher and friend, will take care of the learning process.

Many little children have an uncanny ability to imitate the sounds around them. Their ack-ack guns or fire sirens can be so realistic as to startle us out of our wits. They reproduce these sounds naturally and with little conscious effort. Take the time to listen thoughtfully, and you will be amazed at the flexibility of their voices, the control they have over them, and the skill with which they use them. Many a trained singer would fail in an attempt to follow such youngsters' vocalizations.

In Roland Hayes's autobiography [3] the author tells of his childhood interest in sound and its influence on his musical career. His father spent a great deal of time wandering through the woods and along the streams. He loved nature, lived close to it, and was able to reproduce any animal call at will. Roland Hayes learned this art as a young lad from his father, and he attributes much of his later success to this early use of his voice. He acquired, naturally, the flexibility and control that most singers have to acquire through years of exacting exercises, and with (he believes) far less strain on his vocal organs. Children have unlimited imagination; their ability to identify themselves with an idea provides sufficient motivation to ac-

[3] *Angel Mo' and Her Son.* Little, Brown.

complish the "impossible." The "how" does not stand in their way. When Roland Hayes's father called a deer, he became a "buck" himself.

Not many have the genius of a Roland Hayes, but there is in children plenty of hidden ability that we grown-ups do not have the wit to see or hear. Listen to a child or a group of children anywhere, in their make-believe play or in their sheer physical exuberance, and you can catch innumerable uses of their voices. Then if you still have little respect for this natural ability of children, try to reproduce some of these sounds yourself!

A fire siren, for example. Musicians work hard to achieve the crescendo and decrescendo that children emit without even trying. The whir of an airplane motor, its gradations of intensity, its rhythmic rise and fall; the call of the bullfrog; the radio and its sound effects—all these and countless others the children can turn on and off at will.

Children's make-believe continually calls upon the use of sound to make their play more realistic. They do not merely imitate: they *become* a steamboat, a train, or an animal at the drop of a hat. The child who will not sing a song beyond the range of his speaking voice will spontaneously produce a high-pitched whistle or horn. With younger children especially, the most effective musical guidance may come in connection with this type of play. Recognition and encouragement of it, and *sometimes* participation in it, provide a real opportunity for furthering children's interest in sound.

What parent or teacher has not at some time been driven to exasperation by the incessant "click-clack-clucking" that children make with their mouths? This particular form of recreation has a way of turning up at rest or meal time, and it has a higher rate of contagion than any other childhood disease yet known. A design for tormenting grown-ups? Yes, it may be, for any smart youngster who gets such a reaction will not miss an opportunity to make it just that. But for the child it is, essentially, *fun* to be able to do all these tricks, and he is constantly discovering new and strange noises he can make. We ask children to stop, tell them it is time to rest or time to eat, and not the time for such monkeyshines—that they can pursue this activity later. We have a right to make this request, but *too, too* often we forget about the later time, ourselves. And since these children want someone to listen to them (that being nine-tenths of the fun), we must do our share and take time out to pay attention and *experiment with them.*

In writing of his childhood, Stravinsky says: "One of my earliest memories of sound will seem somewhat odd. It was in the country, where my parents, like most people of their class, spent the summer with their children. I can see it now. An enormous peasant seated on the stump of a tree. . . . He was dumb, but he had a way of clicking his tongue very noisily, and the children were afraid of him. So was I. But curiosity used to triumph over fear. The children would gather round him. Then, to amuse them, he would begin to sing. This song was composed of two syllables, the only ones he could pronounce. They were devoid of any meaning, but he made them alternate with incredible dexterity in a very rapid tempo. He used to accompany this clucking in the following way: pressing the palm of his right hand under his left armpit, he would work his left arm with a rapid movement, making it press on the right hand. From beneath the shirt he extracted a succession of sounds which were somewhat dubious but very rhythmic, and which might be euphemistically described as resounding kisses. This amused me beyond words, and at home, I set myself with zeal to imitate this music—so often and so successfully that I was forbidden to indulge in such an indecent accompaniment."[4]

One little group of five-year-olds made up a "sympathy" (as Miguel called it) by combining their "cluckings"! It was in three "movements": in the first, sounds were made with their mouths wide open; in the second, sounds were made with their mouths partly closed; and a combination of the two with clapping hands constituted the finale!

What do we do about this ability, especially in our schools? We clamp down on it and try to teach our children "music." We give them a course of study that has been logically worked out—simple and harmless, but usually too anemic to hold children's interest. We are blind to the vigor and vitality of the music children have within themselves. Many a youngster is labeled an "out-of-tune" and is the despair of the conscientious teacher or parent. How about turning the tables, how would it be if we ourselves got in tune with the "out-of-tune"? We might well consider Ruskin's idea: that the only way to help others is to first find out what they have been trying to do for themselves, and then proceed to help them do it better.

One of these "out-of-tunes" was five-year-old Mary. When she sang with other children, she never seemed to be able to stay with them. She had a sweet, lovely voice to which she consciously listened when she sang, and the thoughtful way she used it and her feeling around for a pleasant effect in sound restrained us from urging her to try to sing on the same pitch as the rest of us. One day, while we were singing *Ach du lieber Augustin,* Mary's voice suddenly came through clear and steady. She was singing a third higher than the group, and she was able to go through to the end. Her eyes shone with delight—she had hit the spot that satisfied her and gave her a

[4] *Stravinsky, an Autobiography*. Simon and Schuster.

thrill, and "the moment of passage from disturbance into harmony is that of intensest life." [5]

Of course, Mary could easily sing on the same pitch as the others if she wished; her mother told us that she sang a great deal at home. It happened, however, that at the time she started to school she was interested in singing in a different way and—as children so often do—she had accidentally tumbled into a significant musical experience. She would wait until the song was started, then she would feel around with her voice until she found a comfortable place.

If Mary had been placed in an "out-of-tune" group or been compelled by adult pressure to sing on the same pitch, not only she but the entire group would have lost something. For this episode offered an ideal opportunity for teaching them about two-part singing. They had come upon an important aspect of music. As they all tried to sing Mary's way (with varying degrees of success), they experienced and recognized —at five years of age—the essential element of harmony. This was therefore the time for them to be told that when different sounds sound well together, we call it harmony. We did not care whether or not they remembered the word—though most of them did; but we "harmonized" off and on throughout the year. Most of this experimentation went on informally on the playground, during the work period, and at home. Singing simple two-part rounds with an adult supporting each part helped to enlarge experience and give much pleasure.

Again let us listen to children. Two-year-old Jonathan was riding high on his father's shoulders, one summer day, on a walk around the lake. "Ooh!" he squealed, surprised and startled, as his head was brushed by a low branch. "Ooh!" his father called back, so quickly that Jonathan forgot his fright in his enjoyment of this new game. Father found himself going

[5] John Dewey. *Art As Experience*. Minton, Balch.

back and forth under the trees at the young man's demand, so that more "oohs" would be forthcoming. And even though their pitch was occasionally varied, Jonathan was able to reproduce the call every time.

Several days later, a cuckoo clock arrived at Jonathan's home. But he was disappointed by the cuckoo's unpredictability: it simply would not "cuckoo" when he wanted it to, and usually when it did perform he was not near by. After a few frustrated days, Jonathan was observed one morning standing in front of the clock and calling repeatedly: "Cuckoo, cuckoo, cuckoo!" It was so like the clock that his mother found the place on the piano in exact tune with Jonathan's voice, and later, when the clock struck the hour, she discovered that he had imitated it exactly in pitch and interval.

Perhaps this was an accident, but it was no accident that Jonathan could usually find some member of the family to play back and forth with him. On rainy days he and his older sister used to love playing a singing "question and answer" game, the long hall between their rooms being an excellent conductor for their voices.

We are told [6] that the artist Artur Rubinstein used only "song language" until after he was three years old, refusing to tell what he wanted or to call on other members of the family except in a singing voice. It is just as natural for little children to relate their doings in this way as in any other, and we find them doing it continually. They sing about their play, washing their hands, going to bed, getting dressed—in fact, about everything they do. Unfortunately, but for obvious reasons, they lose this natural ability as they grow older; for children do what others do, and other people do not go around singing in this fashion.

[6] Amram Scheinfeld. *Youth and Heredity.* Stokes.

We have described a few, a very few, of the many ways in which little children use their voices. What can we do, as we live with them, that will insure the maximum of enjoyment and learning from these experiences? What guidance can we give, in the home and in the school, that will best contribute to their musical education? For music in these early years *is not a matter of half-hour lessons or music periods; it is part of children's everyday life*. They use it in a functional way and, unless we have a broad conception of music, we are likely to "educate" it out of them.

First of all, we must have confidence in ourselves, and must have respect for the music that is in us. We must blow away the air of mystery with which it is surrounded for many of the uninitiated. This, of course, does not imply shutting our ears to new and unfamiliar experiences. But no one is utterly devoid of music in some form or another. It is contagious; if we feel the need for it, then those who live with us will not go untouched by it. If we are trained musicians, so much the better, provided we are truly broadminded, and flexible in our use of it.

If we provide for children, at home and at school, a simple, happy environment and freedom to use it, our first effective piece of guidance is accomplished. Children also need some form of recognition of what they are doing. This may be only a smile in passing, or a friendly interest, or, if in a group, help in finding a quiet spot where they can *hear* what they are doing.

At times, our actual participation in what a child is doing may be exactly what is needed. That participation may take the form of following his lead entirely, or we may feel that the time is ripe for helping him see the next step ahead. Whether we do this or not depends essentially on our sensitivity—on our perception of his readiness for something more. If he loses interest because of our participation, we have taught him nothing; but if we do not attempt such participation we may miss a rare opportunity to plant a greater interest in him. Sometimes, in our desire not to overstimulate children, we do not live up to the possibilities they have. Children are constantly reaching out for more, and if it is not given them "problems" may turn up.

Making a child aware of what he is doing or has done is part of the learning process. If he can repeat at will what has happened, he has taken a step forward. The group's introduction to harmony that started with Mary's experimenting is an example.

Many opportunities for this type of guidance occur in a child's make-believe play. "This is the way your train whistle sounds," we may say, imitating his voice. Going a little farther, we may sound our whistle on a different pitch or with a change of intensity. "Listen to mine—it is far away." He will enjoy this game and gain much from it provided it is carried on in a spirit of play.

If we are not musicians, we should familiarize ourselves with the fundamental elements of music. In recent years, a number of excellent books about music have been written for the layman. They are interesting and easy to read, and they open up to the reader many of the "mysteries" of music.

Better still, if we can find the time and an understanding teacher, we should plan to spend half an hour a week with him, and at least a few minutes a day with ourselves, in exploring the world of sound. No matter what instrument is our choice—piano, voice, guitar, harmonica, or drums—we shall get many a thrill, and this may be exactly the relaxation we need to bring down our blood pressure or unjangle our nerves.

2

CHILDREN AND INSTRUMENTS

In play with sound, children use not only their voices but also objects that they find around them. All too soon for Mother, the baby discovers that dropping things out of his crib or carriage is great fun. Of course, he enjoys the attention he gets when his plaything is picked up and given back to him, but he also likes the sound it makes when it hits the floor. It is only we grown-ups who tire of this game, and in order to escape so much bending exercise we think up other ways of satisfying the child without wearing ourselves out. So we tie spoons, clothespins, metal cups—in fact, anything at hand—to the sides of his crib or his high chair so that he can toss them about and retrieve them at will. For him, it is not quite so much fun as having grown-ups do his bidding, but he will accept it, and will entertain himself for a long time.

Even when the baby is still in his carriage, we can begin to think about making it possible for him to play with and hear a variety of sounds. We may not be able to go so far as Montaigne's father, who had his son awakened every morning with some instrument in the hope that this practice would influence his character and disposition! But every home has many possibilities if we open our ears to them. One father whose job it was to brush up the crumbs around the family dining table decided that the family needed a new dust pan and announced that he would buy it on his way home from work. His choice was determined not by size, cost, color, or even durability, but by the fact that it pleased his ears as he tapped on it.

Pleasant-sounding rattles and different types of bells are always enjoyed by the little child. Tiny bells sewed securely on a piece of elastic or tape that can be slipped over the wrist are lots of fun. Sound boxes can be made by putting different articles in boxes small enough to be handled easily by the child, and then glueing or nailing on the tops. One nursery-school teacher used little toy wooden kegs for this purpose. After putting nails in one, dried beans in another, and so on, she screwed on the tops, which had previously been brushed with glue.

It would indeed be a hardhearted mother who refused to let Junior investigate the kitchen pots and pans, and she would miss a lot of fun if she did not occasionally sit down and play with him. Even if she has little time and must keep close to her work, she can at least pay attention to this sound-making, for the toddler has ten times the fun if he knows that someone is enjoying it with him.

And right here is an excellent chance to help the child learn more about sound. Instead of asking him not to make such a racket with his spoons and pans, give him a stick that is padded a little at the end. He cannot strike a pan lightly—and besides, he doesn't want to; but the padded stick will produce a pleasanter sound even if he uses the same force in striking with it. (We should never miss an opportunity to substitute a pleasant for an unpleasant sound *provided this does not interfere with the child's play.*) He will probably prefer a loud crash, but we hope that he will gradually get interested in the *differences* in sound. It will be less confusing to him and his interest will last longer if he uses only a few pans at a time, to say nothing of how much easier it will be on Mother! But also see that from time to time he has a change in the number and size of pans.

Helping children to be *alert to the similarities and differences in sounds* is one of the ways we can guide this early interest. As a child plays on a pan, Mother may listen and ask if she, too, may have a turn. Then picking up his pan and tapping it *his* way, she can say: "Listen—this is the way your pan sounded when you played on it." Or again, she may pick up a utensil of another size for herself and tap it, asking the child to notice the difference between the two pans.

If we listen, we shall find that it is not long before a child can repeat the sound he makes with a certain regularity. At first there is no conscious attempt on his part to do this, but he falls into it during the course of his play because he likes it, and he keeps repeating it. Even as simple a bit as "tap-tap" repeated regularly is a rhythmic pattern, and when he can consciously produce this at will, learning has taken place. We can show our interest in what he is doing and help him be more aware of it by repeating what he has done. We should not hurry this stage of playing *his way,* for sometimes in our eagerness to go ahead we expect the child to listen to *our way* before he is ready. Then he loses interest.

An assortment of mixing bowls can produce lovely sounds. (Obviously, it is necessary to wait until the child is old enough to have attained a certain amount of control over his experimentation before putting these at his disposal.) The kind of shoe tree that is tipped by a wooden ball makes an ideal tapper; the steel body is flexible and makes a pleasanter sound when it strikes the bowl than does a rigid stick. Other members of the family will enjoy playing on these bowls, and perhaps they will be able to collect a set of bowls whose various tones enable them to be arranged in scale sequence, and so lend themselves to playing simple melodies. "Tuned" water glasses or bottles are often used in this way as a substitute for a piano, but they are not recommended for very little children because they break too easily.

Another typical sound play that children enjoy is achieved by running a stick along a fence. They like the feel of the stick's vibration as it goes fast or slow, and they play with varying intensities of sound as well as with gradations of rhythm.

In the characteristic sound plays just discussed, we have mentioned a few of the many discoveries of children. The reader may find it interesting to go back to his own childhood and recall what he can of his early sound impressions. One person remembers her manipulation of her bedroom door in such a way that it squeaked the first phrase of *Good Night, Ladies*—though unfortunately the family oilcan thwarted her music career! Another remembers his interest in the different sounds made by the train on rainy and on clear nights. Still another recalls as her first sound experience the satisfying lapping of the puppy drinking his milk. And to another, summer vacation brings up an immediate childhood association with the insect chorus in the country.

Even these few memories are sufficient to convince us of the tremendous interest that children have in sound and rhythm. Sound and rhythm are not in themselves music, but they are the stuff music is made of. Children are sound-conscious—acutely sensitive to all of the elements of sounds. If we wish music to have real meaning in their lives, we shall educate *through* this interest.

CHILDREN USE MUSICAL INSTRUMENTS IN EXPERIMENTING WITH SOUND

The choice of instruments for little children and the way in which these are used demand just as much thoughtful consideration as is given to selecting instruments for older children. If we have respect for the learning capacities during these early years—when they are greater than at any other time during life—we shall not be likely to choose just any instrument that pleases our fancy. Most toy instruments have as little intrinsic worth as toy tools or toy cleaning sets, which appeal to the adult because they are cute, little, and inexpensive. But this does not mean that children's instruments need be expensive, for it is a matter not so much of cost as of careful choice.

Drums are among the most satisfactory instruments, and some of the best ones can be made at home. Large cans, wooden mixing bowls, butter tubs, nail kegs, and large barrels can be used. (Little children cannot make these drums alone, but they will love to help other members of the family to make them.) The inner tube of an automobile tire stretched tightly across one end of the tub or barrel gives forth a deep, resounding, primitive sound. Better still is a skin drum head such as can be secured at a musical-instrument supply store; "seconds" are much less expensive and just as satisfactory as new ones. A head made of skin is superior to a rubber one because it is easier to control the sound; when rubber is struck rapidly, the sounds overlap and are muffled. Both kinds, however, will be found useful; in fact, a variety of sizes and shapes of drums will add more interest to children's experimentation.

A pair of "bonga" drums—two small but different-sized drums attached to each other in Siamese fashion—offer an interesting contrast in sound. These are used in many small orchestras and can be bought at instrument stores.

One of the most satisfactory types of commercial drums is the large Chinese tom-tom that can be placed on the floor or on a low table. These drums are strong and sturdy and stand up remarkably well under use. Their pigskin heads seem to be less affected by atmospheric pressure than other kinds of skins.

A pair of regular tympani sticks padded with lamb's wool —they can be bought at a music store—will prove a very worthwhile investment. If it is not possible to get these, they may be made by wrapping the ends of two sticks with firm padding. It is necessary to try out the padding in order to find one that will produce the best sound, for it must be neither too hard nor too soft.

Besides the large drums, there are of course a variety of small ones of the snare and tom-tom type that are usually sold for children's use. They enjoy carrying these around and using them in dramatic play, as in parades and processions. The regulation small boy's parade drum is suspended by a cord around his neck, and swings along in front of him as he walks, making it difficult for him to play on it with any degree of regularity. The Indian tom-tom, made from a tree trunk and small enough to fit under his arm, is much easier to manage. The wooden mixing-bowl drum, in the center of which has been bored a hole large enough for a forefinger to be placed, is also easily handled.

Experience leads us to believe, however, that more thoughtful experimentation is possible when the drum is placed in a convenient position so that the child is free to use both hands in playing. Thus all of his attention is directed toward his playing.

Moreover it allows a freer development of his feeling for rhythm because his body is allowed to move naturally as he plays, and all this, in turn, helps his playing as a whole. Perhaps the best results are obtained when the child is standing and the drum is placed at a level so that his stick or hands will drop on it easily. Or he may prefer to sit down, or kneel, or sit on the floor when using it. In any case, his body should be free and uncramped.

The outdoors is an ideal place for little children to use drums. Their first attempts are sure to be full of vim and vigor, and this is as it should be. We must not ask for control too soon, for they do not want to play "lightly." Remember, too, that a hard stick used vigorously on a drum head can make a very unpleasant sound, whereas a padded stick can be used with full force and yet be free from harshness.

It is a good idea, especially in nursery and kindergarten groups, to set aside for the use of instruments special corners that are off the line of traffic, removed from the noisy activities of wood work or block-building. Then the young musicians are not distracted and can *hear* what they are playing.

Children should be given every opportunity to try out these instruments in their own way. By this we mean *legitimate* experimentation for the purpose of sound- and music-making. Obviously, musical instruments should be respected as such, and not rolled around like balls or pounded with hammers.

Here are some of the things children discover about drums:

1. Not only the head but also the sides and the edges of a drum can be played on.

2. Weather changes the sound of drums, because of its effect on the skin.

3. The sound of the drum comes from the vibration of the head. This vibration can be *felt,* on a large drum, by putting

the hand very close to it as it is played; and *seen,* by putting a small amount of sawdust or sand on the head and watching it move round as the drum is played.

4. Different drums have surprisingly different sounds. After a child is familiar with the sounds of several specific drums, he may enjoy playing a game in which he only listens, trying to decide which drum is being played. This is a good test of ear discrimination and can be made increasingly difficult when the child is ready for it.

5. The same drum head sounds different when struck at different places. Usually a spot near the side produces a better effect than does the exact center.

6. The hands may be used in various ways to play a drum, and some drums respond better to hands than to sticks.

7. Children can gradually be helped to *feel* and *hear* that when a sound is "pulled out" of the drum it is much better than when "beaten in."

8. Drums may be played loud or soft, fast or slow. Much experimentation is possible not only with rhythm and intensity but also with combinations of drums.

It will not be long before a child falls into a regular rhythm when playing on a drum, and we must be sure to let this happen naturally. The opportunity comes when we hear it happen; we can then register it for him by repeating what he has done or by helping him repeat it. When he has established a rhythm, he may enjoy having us play with him, either on another drum or on his, provided we do not run away with the show. If he can maintain a steady rhythm, it is fun to pick it up, carry it along with one hand, and improvise a secondary rhythm with the other. This relieves the monotony of the steady beat and gives the child a new experience; sometimes he will be able to take over the "orchestration" while we provide the primary rhythm.

Another interesting time can be had by placing four or five drums at varying distances from each other in a circular formation, leaving enough space in the center so that the child can move freely from one instrument to another. The rhythm produced as he moves from one to the other, dropping the end of his stick (or using his hand) on each instrument in turn, is determined by the placement of the drums. The movement of the body provides the primary rhythm, and the instruments the secondary one. This type of experimentation has endless possibilities in contrasts of sound and rhythm, and grown-ups will enjoy it too. It is just another way of discovering and developing into form the rhythm that we have in us, instead of approaching rhythm from the mechanical end of "counting out."

(Speaking of adults, especially those who do not play an instrument, there is no group of instruments that offers such a thoroughly good time as the percussion. Some of the "unmusical" faculty members of one of our large eastern colleges have had a rip-roaring time the last few years in a percussion orchestra. Great music is not the aim nor the result, but there is a tremendous amount of "self-expression" and fun in it.)

With little children, we are concerned with the individual use of instruments. They like to be near adults or other children, but each one likes to play his own way, whatever activity he may be engaged in. As they grow older, however, they become more interested in playing with others. In music, as in any other activity, this stage cannot be hurried. Usually between the ages of five and six, however, children begin to show interest in playing in a small *informal* group. Occasionally one of their number has sufficient initiative and ability to hold the group together. At other times an older person is needed to help organize their ideas, and supplement these if it is felt that the time is ripe.

The music corner of an outdoor playground lends itself particularly well to this first group playing; there the other children are not disturbed and the players are much freer to experiment with sound than they would be indoors.

Here is a typical example of the way in which group interest may develop and be enriched by guidance. The first important thing is to see that the interested children are protected from the noisy play of the rest of the group. Much of the time children will be sufficient unto themselves, but they like to know that a grown-up is interested. You can always tell when you can add to what they are doing.

A group of three five-year-olds had been playing off and on together every morning for a week. They came to school early each day to help carry the drums to the playground, but especially to get a first turn in playing them. One day we heard them chanting as they played, in well-accented rhythm: "You better watch out for your whole life!" It kept getting louder and louder, and it seemed that it would never stop. Finally we suggested that music changes, has different parts, and that in an orchestra the instruments sometimes take turns in playing. Perhaps they might try something like that, using their voices part of the time and instruments part of the time?

The shoutings, however, went on as before, only with more vigor and enthusiasm, and the next day's performance was the same except that almost all the rest of the group had joined in! Evidently the moment of readiness for the next step was not at hand.

On the third day, however, there was a variation in intensity, and just a beginning of a feeling for form. The children were really thinking about what they were doing; they experimented in various ways (sometimes with an adult helping and again by themselves), and after three days came through with the following arrangement.

DRUMS AND VOICES:
You better watch out for your whole life!
You better watch out for your whole life!
VOICES ALONE:
Better watch out—better watch out!
Better watch out—better watch out!
VOICES ALONE (hushed):
Shoo, shoo, shoo, shoo,
Shoo, shoo, shoo . . .
DRUMS AND VOICES:
You better watch out for your whole life!
VOICES SHOUTING (finale):
Watch out!

As the year went on, other instruments were *gradually* made available to the children but not until we felt that these instruments would enlarge their musical interests. For example, as the children became conscious of climax as part of form, a large gong suspended on a stand was given them. When we felt they would profit by new contrasts in sound, Korean temple bells (hollow wooden bells) were introduced. Placed on a table covered with a mat, they gave out a pleasant, "liquid" sound when tapped with a striker that had a hard rubber tip. Gourd rattles were used frequently, especially by the dancing members of the group, for very often the players were joined by dancers.

In the beginning these instruments were used without a piano, but later on we occasionally added a piano accompani-

Investigating the sounds kitchen pots and pans make

The Chinese tom-tom is in a convenient position for the child to play it freely with both hands

Making up a melody on the resonator bells

Putting sounds and rhythms together

ment in the form of simple improvised chords or music that would fit into the children's plan. In working with a group we sometimes find it helpful to ask one child to start playing, the others listening until he has established his rhythm, then each one joining in when he *feels* the music would sound better by the addition of his instrument. Gradually, a feeling for the whole is built up, and children begin to plan ahead, and to repeat what they have already done. Basic, however, to this type of group work is *long and unhurried time for individual use of instruments*—that is, if we are working honestly for children's progressive music development and not simply for products. The very different kinds of music that result depend on what instrument and what child take the lead.

This is the way children can work in a truly creative way with sound and rhythm. It is a slow process, but a rewarding one—at times even a thrilling one. We believe that the limitations lie in us grown-ups rather than in the children—in our inability to find material for music in the great variety of sounds that children make.

After the children have worked for some time with instruments, they enjoy "orchestrating" music that is played for them; this becomes a thoughtful musical experience—not an occasion for merely beating time. Often they work out a plan with their instruments and then ask for music to supplement or re-enforce it. It is not uncommon for a child to go to the piano and either "improvise" the music himself or play enough to show us the character of the music he wishes to have.

But this is only *one* of the ways in which children develop musically through the use of instruments. Unfortunately, we have found that all too frequently the procedure is to tie up the children's first experimentation with ready-made music—either by chanting nursery rhymes or by piano music. Children enjoy it, and there is every reason why they should, because it is easier for them to depend on what is outside of them than to try out their own ideas. Too often, however, keeping time is the only musical aspect of the experience, and the awareness of sound and the rhythm of the whole is neglected.

Other instruments that children frequently use in groups are the triangle, the tambourine, cymbals, and bells. Together with drums, these are usually associated with "rhythm bands." From time to time we read of the musical achievement of a group of little tots who give a rhythm band show under the "leadership" of a young prodigy who stands on a podium and conducts. Fond parents applaud, and all (except the prodigy's mamma) secretly envy the genius of the leader. This may be a musical experience for the children who participate (though we doubt it), but it most certainly is not a healthy emotional experience. The children who are the best players always get the important instruments, and the ones who need help the most are kept in the background with instruments that are not too obvious. Not that there may not be satisfaction to some in just being in a group; but it has been the unhappy experience of hundreds of thoughtful teachers that the frustrations and disappointments of the shy child as well as of the less skilled (to say nothing of what happens to the leader's ego) have far outweighed any compensations inherent in this kind of performance.

Yes, it is possible to train any group of little children to keep time, and they will accept a plan laid down from above. Whether or not it is sound procedure from the standpoint of child development and of musical development is another question. Certainly the value of a rhythm band in training children to keep time to music can be discounted. If children have plenty of opportunity to use their bodies in a free and rhythmic way, if they have frequent use of instruments individually and in small groups, and—above all—if they are relaxed and free of tension, then keeping time is something we need not train them to do. We can't keep them from doing it! It is as natural to them as running and jumping.

The instruments generally used in a rhythm band can be used by children in a creative way, as and when the need for them is evident. Tambourines are fun to play and to dance with; they provide the crashes of sound so loved by youngsters. Bells offer another contrast. The triangle is a gentle instrument, but because of its swinging movement it is not so easy to play. As for cymbals, we prefer a gong or a cymbal struck with a tympani stick to the uncertain effect produced by the crashing of two cymbals together. The latter are difficult for a little child to play, calling for care and skill if good results are to be obtained.

Tonal instruments that give opportunity for melodic experimentation offer still another type of musical experience for children. Among these are a few that are easily moved from place to place. One of the most satisfactory portable instruments is a set of "resonator bells" made of metal bars attached to blocks of wood. When struck with a hammer the bars produce an unusually lovely sound. One of the advantages is that each block is separate; a little child may be given only a few at a time, or even one if that seems better. The resonator bells are accurately tuned to the diatonic scale and are constructed in such a way that it is well-nigh impossible for them to get out of tune.

When these blocks are to be used, it is important that they be placed in correct scale sequence, with the lowest tone to the left, corresponding to the arrangement of the piano keyboard.

A set of eight comes in a box designed to hold them, and it is better to leave them in this box when playing them, since they will thus not easily get out of correct order. If only 1-2-3 or 1-2-3-4-5 of the scale is given to the child first, it is a good plan to find a box into which either of these groups will fit snugly.

Each child will use these blocks in his own way, and should be left free to do so. His first playing is likely to be haphazard, but soon he will discover certain tonal arrangements and sequences, such as thirds, high and low, or various rhythmic patterns. Occasionally he will enjoy having someone repeat to him what he has just played, or he may like to take a turn repeating what someone else has played.

We should *let his ear be his guide* when he begins to try out familiar melodies. He will find that not all of the songs he knows will fit on these blocks, since their range is limited, but there are many songs within the range of the five tones or the eight tones in the set, and a few use only three tones. We can encourage him to sing along with his playing if that seems to help him to find the tune. We should not, however, urge him too much to play songs that he already knows, for one of the values of this instrument is that it encourages him to make up his own melodies. Both of these experiences are important, but unless we show continued interest in his own inventions, he is likely to give them up. One of the things we can help him learn is that if the tip of the hammer is *dropped* on the bar, a much more musical tone will result than if the bar is *struck*. Again, we cannot ask for this control too soon, for it is not so easy as it looks, but since we are concerned, in musical guidance, with acquainting a child with pleasant rather than unpleasant sounds, it is well to encourage it whenever the time is opportune.

For children the resonator bells are recommended rather

than the small marimba or the xylophone because they have a larger striking surface, they are not so close together as the bars on a xylophone, and they have an excellent tone quality. Little children's lack of motor co-ordination makes it hard for them to play on an instrument in which the tones are close together. If a substitute for the tone blocks has to be used, it should be well constructed and accurate.

Tuned bells attached to a standard make a delightful instrument. Though fairly expensive, they are practically indestructible—an excellent investment for a school, especially when pianos are not available. They can be used by a number of groups. There are two types: One is in regulation bell shape; the other is round and flat, like an old-fashioned doorbell. They are screwed to a standard and are easily removed, so that the number of bells can be limited for the younger children. If one end of the tapper is attached by a long string to the standard, it will be on hand when needed.

Bowls, tuned glasses, and bottles have been mentioned as suitable for older children. If the glasses are placed on a piece of felt in a long, narrow tray, they can be moved about easily. Sometimes, if one is patient and has a good ear, it is possible to select a set of glasses that are tuned to the scale, making it unnecessary to tune them by pouring water in. Tuning glasses is good training, and its value is evident for older children, but it cannot be done unless one has a reliable ear, or can check with another instrument. Corked bottles suspended from a stand are, for purposes of accurate pitch, more satisfactory than open glasses, since the water in the glasses evaporates quickly and they get out of tune.

Tonal instruments are used individually by the younger children, since it is beyond their ability to play melodically in groups as do older children. It is always of first importance that these instruments be accurately tuned, because *there is no substitute for correct tonal relationship*. They offer interesting possibilities in experimenting with melody and with similarities and differences of pitch. Just before Christmas, four-year-old Dorothy, taking off her snow suit in the hall, overheard us arranging the tone blocks and testing them by playing down the scale. As she came into the room, she said: "That sounded like a candlelight song, but it wasn't quite the same." She had heard part of a Christmas carol service the day before, and when we played the first phrase of *Joy to the world, the Lord is come,* her eyes danced with the thrill of recognition; she had caught the melodic progression even though the rhythm was different.

When children enjoy finding the same pitch of a tone on another instrument, they begin to be ear-conscious of an instrument's timbre as well as of intervals—the distance from one tone to another. All of these tonal instruments give excellent ear training, and that is the foundation of a sound musical education.

The use of these instruments has been described at length, even at the risk of being repetitious, because it is the way they are used that determines their musical benefit. Too often instruments are placed in the child's environment, and no more attention is paid them. His growth through them is hit or miss, and many opportunities for musical development are not even recognized. What music occurs is accidental, and remains so. When music education is thought to begin with piano lessons, there is no appreciation of the value inherent in these earlier experiences. Musical impressions gained during children's pliable early years have a way of sticking, and all during their lives a feeling of at-homeness is never entirely lost. Later on, music lessons will have more meaning if this important early training is recognized at its true worth.

Good portable instruments are not inexpensive and many families are unable to afford them. There is no reason, however, why the school or public library of a community should not have a collection available for children's use. The future of our schools lies in a closer bond with the community, and such a service would be a valuable one. School libraries lend books, some of them offering these over the summer vacation. Why could not a similar privilege be extended in the lending of musical instruments for the use of little children? If the school could not, perhaps the public library, or a church, or the community center might be interested in trying it out. The financial outlay would be comparatively small, and there are many ways of raising money; but the returns in satisfaction for children, especially those who have no instruments in their homes, would be great.

SUGGESTED READING

Satis Coleman. *The Drum Book*. John Day
Bernard F. Mason. *Drums, Tomtoms and Rattles*. Barnes

3

THE PIANO

THE PIANO is a grand and glorious instrument, and fortunate is the person who can make it speak in a grand and glorious way. Is there anyone who at one time or another has not felt the urge to sit down and pour out through its sounds the pent-up feelings that have a way of gathering in all of us? Some people are "naturals"—have never known that once they could not play. Others have achieved the ability to make the instrument do their bidding through long and laborious study. The vast majority of people, however, are shut off from this form of self-expression.

Even though we grown-ups may not accept this frustration graciously, at least we can understand it. But when little children suddenly realize that "taking piano lessons" does not guarantee within a reasonable length of time (i.e., a short time) to put them in complete control of the instrument, they are confronted with one of the first great disappointments of their lives. They, too, have big feelings and big emotions, and there are many times when picking out "Mary Had a Little Lamb" in no way measures up to the size of what is pushing within them.

For children, a piano is a sound-making instrument, not an

object to which one transfers notes read from a printed page. Children do not wait to play the piano until they can read notes, any more than they wait to talk until they can read the printed word. In both cases they learn through their ears. When they are old enough, they are only too ready to learn to read from the printed page, either in music or in books.

Children are curious about a piano—all parts of it, inside and out—and nothing else offers them so much fun as exploring it. The piano is, of course, a precious instrument and one cannot afford to have disastrous things happen to it. But there are many things children can find out about its workings, under proper supervision, and not only will no harm be done to the piano, but the children's interest in music will be tremendously enhanced.

Not long ago Susan's mother, a concert pianist, paid us an unexpected visit at school. We had asked her many times to come and play for us, but she is a busy woman. At last, however, she found a spare half-hour during a morning. For several days before her visit, the children had been spending considerable time investigating the inside of the piano, and when she came into the room half a dozen of them were around it, standing on chairs, tables, or anything available so as to get as close as possible to the strings and the sounding board.

Diana had the advantage of being near the deep end, and could "strum" the long strings and make the biggest sound; several were playing on the keyboard and watching the hammers; another was plucking the upper strings. Confusion —yes, plenty of it—and besides, no one could hear the sound he himself was making. So we suggested that each person take a turn so that he could *listen to his own music*. Susan's mother was as excited over what was happening as the children were, and soon she sat down at the keyboard to control the duration of the sound by the pedal. She had her turn, too—for, said she, "I have played the piano since I was a little girl, but I have never played the strings!"—and she was thrilled by the strange and lovely sounds. One of the boys said: "Her music is 'banshee' music, just like what I heard on the radio!"

Just before Susan's mother left she played a Bach gavotte, but this time the music was not so much heard as watched, for the children were intrigued by seeing the hammers bob up and down on the strings. When she said good-by she declared that never in her life had she spent such an enjoyable half-hour, or such a profitable one musically.

Time and again during the year the children experiment with the inside of the piano, always under adult supervision since it is important for them to learn to use it carefully and thoughtfully. They look forward eagerly to the coming of the piano tuner and listen while he works; and of course there is always someone to help him decide whether he has just the right pitch! Usually, a few of the children stay by until the end; most of them, being five-year-olds, go back and forth to the piano from their work and play; but not one but has contact with some aspect of the experience. Our tuner, a friendly person, always takes time to answer questions; there usually aren't many, for the children's own observations supply the answers. He shows them how the tuning fork is used, and each child has a chance to try it.

There is no way of measuring what the children thus learn about the piano during the year, for we do not quiz them. But if enthusiastic interest, thoughtful listening, and experimentation are any indications, we venture to guess that the piano's Crossley rating is near the top.

The children are given many unhurried opportunities to try out and observe; then their questions are answered simply and directly; and, finally, new information is offered when the time is opportune. Words and names are not flung at them, but neither are these withheld when needed. That children pick up far more than we are aware of is evidenced by reports of their conversations at home and by overhearing their talk among themselves.

Here are some of the things children discover about the piano:

The vibration of the string produces the sound. The string is made to vibrate by the hammers dropping on it. Plucking the string will also make it vibrate.

Strings of different lengths produce different sounds. We call the sounds made by the short strings "high," and those made by the long strings "low."

The length or duration of the sound can be controlled by the pedal.

When the strings are played in certain ways they remind us of other sounds—bombers, wind, motors, airplanes, witches.

The vibration of the strings can be seen by placing a pencil or piece of paper on them, and then playing them from the keyboard.

Strings are made of various materials: some are copper, some steel. Some are thicker than others.

In the upper register of the piano the hammer falls on three strings at once; in the lower register, on only one at a time.

Intensities and duration of sounds may be experimented with by using the pedals, by closing and opening the top, and by using the hands with varying degrees of pressure.

One of the recent outcomes of our children's experimentation with the piano was continued interest in the physics of sound. The kindergarten room is very large, and—being flanked on three sides by seventeen windows reaching from ceiling to floor—is well known (among adults) for its echoes. One day Anna objected strongly to the shouting of a group of boys who were playing war, saying that the noise hurt her ears. She couldn't understand why they did not wait until they were outdoors to play war. This same group of boys had been much interested in the piano experience, so we thought they might like to know something about the acoustics of the room. We called the children for a meeting and told them of Anna's complaint, and most of them agreed that it had been very noisy. Then we tried the following experiment.

We told the boys that we were going to *listen* while they played war again, and asked them to "shoot their guns" just as before. After the enemy had been annihilated, we all went downstairs to the soundproofed cafeteria (then, in mid-morning, not in use) and asked the boys to continue their war while we *listened* again. The listeners immediately noticed the difference in sound. Then we pointed to the ceiling and told them that much of the noise was absorbed by it, whereas in our own room the ceiling was hard and had no little holes in it, and there were many glass windows which stopped the sound so that it remained in the room.

Then we went to the roof and repeated the experiment. We did not need to ask what happened to the sound up there, for one youngster volunteered the information that "it just goes up into the sky, and then away out into the ocean and drowns!"

When we went back to our room, we showed the children a soundproof block that had been given to us some time before. They could see the tiny perforations that absorb the sound. The next day, we experimented by listening to the tick of a watch, first placing a piece of porous cloth between it and the child's ear, then wetting a similar piece of cloth and using it in the same way. Water closed the holes of the cloth, and the sound of the watch tick was reduced. By using a strong magnifying glass, the children could see for themselves the differences in the cloth.[1]

Again a comparison of children's curiosities with those of certain adults may be of interest to the reader. Hull tells us in his life of Scriabin that the composer "derived all harmony from 'nature's harmonic chord,' and thus carried the science of sound triumphantly into the regions of art."[2] Cowell and Stokowski are both well known for their excursions into the science of sound as it relates to music.

Far be it from us to suggest that we have any musical prodigies in our group, or that there is a moral to this story so far as the noise-making proclivities of youngsters are concerned. Little boys, and little girls too, aren't made to be quiet, but perhaps a request for quieter play in a room where others are annoyed by it might seem to them just a little less arbitrary when they understand a tiny bit about what happens to the sound made by their voices. The mother of one of our "highly developed" noise-makers reported one day that after she had asked Jack to be quieter at home, he responded with exasperation: "Why don't you give me a soundproofed room? Then you wouldn't hear me!"

Other opportunities for exploring sound occur from time to time. For example, when Louise's mother brought her 'cello to school to play for us, we observed the difference in sounds when she played with the peg on the bare floor, and when it was placed on a thick rubber pad; also, what happened when the mute was used.

Not only the inside of the piano but also the piano keyboard

[1] Wilmer Bartholomew. *Acoustics of Music.* Prentice-Hall.
[2] A. Eaglefield Hull. *A Great Russian Tone-Poet: Scriabin.*

presents endless ways of experimenting with sound. No wonder children delight in playing on it; high or low, tiny or big, soft or loud, dissonances or pleasing sounds—all respond to their immediate control. Even the tiny baby on his mother's lap can satisfy his urge for sound-making.

"But I will not have my children banging on the piano," said the musician-father of two little children recently. "When they are old enough, I'll see that they have lessons from the best teacher available, and until then they can listen to music and learn to appreciate it."

What this father fails to see is that there is a vast difference between uncontrolled, haphazard banging on a keyboard, and thoughtful experimentation with it, even though the results may sound alike. In one case the child is not really interested nor even thinking about what he is doing; in the other, he is making a *conscious* effort to produce sounds that satisfy him. Or, to put it simply, it is the difference between not using his ears and using them. Surely no thoughtful person could call this second kind of playing "banging." The sounds produced may not please him, but plenty of published music does not please either. In writing about sound in *Music for All of Us,* Stokowski says: "All sound can be music to some—to them every sound has some kind of tonal design, no matter how irregular." [3] Is it not possible, then, for us to see in this early keyboard curiosity an opportunity for constructive guidance, and is this not far better than to prohibit the child's investigations?

Perhaps if we enumerate some of the ways in which little children use the keyboard, we may see more clearly the elements of music inherent in this type of sound-making.

[3] Leopold Stokowski. *Music for All of Us.* Simon and Schuster.

GROUPS OF KEYS. Playing the piano with the whole hand or even with the forearm is one of the ways in which very little children experiment. This frequently tends toward rhythmic as well as sound play, and, by the way, this use of the keyboard is not confined to children. One of our well-known modern composers and pianists, Henry Cowell, often uses his forearm in playing "tone clusters," and he also produces unusual and very beautiful music by playing on the strings. He has an exquisite sensitivity to sounds and a unique approach to their production, plus fine creative powers and able musicianship.

BLACK KEYS. Quiet, sensitive, three-year-old Timothy used the school piano a great deal, and the interesting thing about his playing was that he used the black keys exclusively. No one had told him to do this, but apparently these sounds pleased and satisfied him, so he stuck to them. Timothy's mother was musical, and he was accustomed to hearing good music at home; even at the age of three he showed unusual discrimination in his appreciation of music. In talking with his parents, we all came to the conclusion that the way he used the piano was only another evidence of his discrimination, for in using only the black keys (the pentatonic scale), he encountered no dissonances. We are told that Mozart at the age of three showed a "pronounced liking for concords and [an] aversion [to] discords. He gave joyous gurgles when he put down a satisfying third." [4]

INTERVALS AND RHYTHMIC PATTERNS. Five-year-old Mary liked music and hung around the piano when the children were using it. We noticed, however, that she never played, and when

[4] Dyneley Hussey. *Wolfgang Amade Mozart.* Routledge.

we urged her to take a turn she refused, saying that she did not know how to play. This was a shock to us, for in all our experience, we had never met a little child who had even the shadow of a doubt that he could play! There was no lack of volunteers to help Mary, but still she held back. Finally she turned to us and said, "You show me how to play *Frère Jacques.*" We played it for her twice, at the same time saying: "You can easily learn how to play that, but there are many more interesting things that you can play. Try playing all over the keyboard." We were especially anxious to have her use the keyboard in her own way, for it was typical of her to wait to be shown how to do things, never using her own imagination and ability. Finally she began to play with one finger, and advanced, key by key, until she had covered the entire keyboard, and then she repeated the whole procedure, this time including the black keys.

By now there was no use for anyone else to try to take a turn, because Mary could not be pulled away. About ten minutes later, she ran over to us excitedly. "Come and listen!" She was playing in thirds (one finger in each hand) up and down, first both notes together, later one after the other in a rocking sort of rhythm. Then she played them in two-four rhythm with the accent in the left hand, and later on she discovered a three-four rhythm, playing the accent on one and the other note on three.

Hardly a day passed that did not find Mary at the piano, experimenting in a variety of rhythmic patterns, in all the intervals, and in unusual harmonic combinations. Frequently we played back to her what she had just done; she would listen carefully and then play it again. Sometimes she would close her eyes, and we would play for her a very short bit, and she would repeat it. This good game worked both ways, and we

"Sounding her way"

Finding out how it works

Children are curious about the piano

got tripped as often as she did. We both found that it helped if we sang the melody as we tried to play it. Since Mary could count accurately, we named the intervals she played, showing her by counting the steps between the tones why they were so called: thirds, fourths, fifths, and so on. After letting her get considerable experience with this we told her to close her eyes and tell us—when we played a third and then an octave—which was a *little* interval and which was a *big* one. She did this accurately and without hesitation.

This delight in harmony is characteristic of many children's experimentation. Grieg reported that at the age of five he was thrilled by "the wonderful mysterious satisfaction with which my arms stretched out to the piano to discover—not a melody—that was far off—no, that there is such a thing as harmony. First a third, then a chord of three notes, then a full chord of four, ending at last with both hands. Oh, joy! a combination of five, the chord of the ninth. When I found that out my happiness knew no bounds."[5]

Mary's interest was so intense that it carried over to the home, and her family decided that it was time to buy a piano. Knowing her mother's love of perfection in all things, we told her very carefully just what Mary had been doing. We urged that Mary be allowed to use the piano in her own way, and that she should not be expected to play tunes all the time. Mary had learned to play a few simple songs by ear, but she was much more eager to do "big things."

Now this story has a moral—for grown-ups. Shortly after the piano arrived in Mary's house, her interest in it began to decrease steadily. Her mother was unable to see any musical value in what Mary had been doing and, determining to waste no time, started to teach her correct fingering, called her experi-

[5] Henry T. Finck. *Grieg and His Music*. John Lane.

mentation silly, and insisted on her practicing scales every day! And in doing this she destroyed her child's curiosity and interest, and especially her enthusiastic persistence in learning.

SOUND EFFECTS. In much of their make-believe play, children supply the necessary sound effects with their own voices, but occasionally they turn to instruments. They may ask an adult to supply the music, but more often than not they are self-sufficient. John was a backward child, graded "slow" by the usual school standards. He followed the lead of others, was friendly and amiable, but lacked the ability to make himself felt in the group. One day, shortly after Hallowe'en, a small group including John were playing pumpkins and asked us to play some "night pumpkin music." "But," we said, "we are not sure what kind of music you need. Could you tell us?" "Oh, I'll show you," said John as he went to the piano and started to play in the lower register. Then he stopped abruptly and asked to have the lights turned off. How could he play night music in a light room?

John's music, in its feeling for weird sound and slow movement, was so completely fitting that there was no question of his showing us what to do; his effect was far superior to anything we could contribute.

This experience proved to be a milestone for John. His imagination had found an outlet, and he achieved recognition by the group. He was constantly called upon to contribute his talent, for talent he had and in no small measure.

PITCH. Ear training is fundamental to a sound music education, and the children's use of the piano can contribute a great deal to this. In pointing out the possibilities for development, we must remind the reader that they are *only possibilities,* and the way in which they are opened up depends entirely on the child's interest and on the guidance or furtherance of that interest.

High and low in music are arbitrary terms, and children have to learn that tones are high or low in relation to a given tone. Middle C is in the middle of the piano, the tones to the right are higher, and the tones to the left are lower. Repeated experiences in playing or singing a middle tone and then a higher or lower one, letting the child decide which each is, will help him to understand this. We must be sure, however, not to stick to middle C as our middle tone, but to use others as well.

After the child has a clear understanding of this, he will be interested in using only his ears in deciding whether the second tone played is higher or lower than the first, and it is important to use wide differences at first. Some children have very acute ears, and it is not long before they can distinguish even a half-tone of difference. This game should be played the other way around, too: let the child take a turn to play, and Mother do the guessing.

Another game that increases awareness of pitch is singing a tone and then finding the same tone on the piano. Several children can enjoy this together, each one taking a turn singing and the others helping to decide when the piano tone matches.

Matching the tones of other instruments, tonal and percussion, with the piano is also good fun. An interesting experiment is to find the corresponding pitch of a drum on the piano on a dry day, and compare it with the pitch on a damp day; or, for an immediate contrast, to use a drum like the Wigman, whose head can be tightened or loosened.

Occasionally children show an interest in the names of piano keys. They will enjoy finding all the C's on the keyboard or all the F's, and so on. After learning the names, they can play a game of closing their eyes, landing on the keyboard with one finger, and naming the key.

MELODIES. Children like to pick out simple melodies by ear, and they should be encouraged to do this, for there is no better ear training possible. "I started piano by my own intuition. There were no lessons, no effort to teach me. With one finger I was always seeking, always trying to find the melodies." This was Paderewski at three years of age.[6] The ease with which some children play a tune in any key they happen to land on arouses jealousy in some of us older people who learned the hard way. They become truly versatile on the keyboard and avoid many of the difficulties that arise later when they read music. Their ears are their guide, and for the average child they are a reliable one. Good music teachers stress playing in many keys from the very beginning.

Many of these first melodies will, we hope, be of the children's own making. Sometimes they will have words but usually they are without. If our ears are quick enough to play back to children their make-up tunes, this will add much pleasure to their experience. They will also play songs that they know or hear others sing, and at times they will run into difficulties. It is important to help them over these hurdles and not let them get discouraged.

Children enjoy hearing the melody of the scale, and in the beginning we must be sure to see that they become scale-conscious *in their ears*—not in terms of letters, numbers, names, or syllables. Here again they can start on any key, letting their ears guide them. (Disregard fingering at the piano.) They will enjoy singing a simple scale song like "As I climbed up

[6] *Memoirs by Ignace Jan Paderewski and Mary Lawton*. Scribner.

the apple tree, A big red apple fell on me"; or "It's fun to see the jolly clown, He shouts 'Hurrah' and tumbles down" in a major key; or "The north wind comes, the north wind goes, But where he lives nobody knows" in a minor key. Some of the older children may make up scale songs, and also they may be interested in distinguishing between songs that go up and down, step by step, and those that skip tones.

MUSIC LESSONS. "When shall I give Alice music lessons, and can you recommend a teacher?" Asked over and over again, this is one of the most difficult questions to answer for the simple reason that there is no one answer. Music lessons might be exactly what six-year-old Ann needs—and an unhappy experience for Alice, even though she shows the same interest as Ann. For children who go to a kindergarten where the teacher is able to give them many experiences in music and movement, or for those who live in a home that encourages and guides their interest, so-called music lessons would seem unnecessary before six years of age. For other children who have neither of these privileges, fifteen or twenty minutes of *musical experiences* with an understanding teacher several times a week should prove very fruitful.

The home will have to be the final judge of whether or not the child is ready for music lessons. Perhaps Mother and Father will not have to worry about making this great decision; it may be taken out of their hands as it was in the case of the parents of little six-year-old Peter Tchaikovsky.

Very early in life he displayed a remarkable ear and quick perception. . . . He could repeat on the piano all that he heard on the orchestration. He found such delight in playing that it was frequently necessary to drag him by force from the instrument.

Afterwards, as the next best substitute, he would take to drumming tunes upon the window panes. One day, while thus engaged, he was so entirely carried away by this dumb show that he broke the glass and cut his hand severely. This accident led his parents to reflect upon the child's incurable tendency and consider the question of his musical education.[7]

The choice of a teacher is of paramount importance, for it is the quality of the relation between teacher and child that determines whether or not the child has a happy and profitable time. We should not choose a teacher simply because she is a concert artist, or because she plays very well. The only sure way to decide whether a certain teacher will bring out the best in the child is to observe that person at work with children. Any honest and sincere teacher is only too happy to offer that opportunity.

What are some of the things, then, that we look for in a teacher? Does she have genuine respect for little children's intelligence, and does she understand them? Is she aware not only of their possibilities, but of their limitations in such matters as short span of attention and inadequate muscular control? Does she have a broad understanding of music and is she flexible in her use of it? Does she see possibilities in children's curiosities about sound? Does she teach by a "system," tying herself and the child to a rigid lesson plan, or is she able to see more immediate and more important possibilities? Is she interested merely in training, or in sound progressive music development? Does she recognize signs of fatigue and lack of interest and proceed intelligently?

These and many more qualifications, depending upon the individual child's need, are essential. Today there *are* teachers

[7] Rosa Newmarch, ed. *The Life and Letters of Peter Ilyitch Tchaikovsky.*

who know and understand children and whose first concern is the child and not music. We should search until we find that person, tell her what we want, and then *be sure* that we do not handicap her by asking for immediate results in terms of performance. The results to be sought after are of a different nature; they are sustained interest in and love of music, eagerness for "music time," creative use of sound and rhythm, and a happy relationship with the music teacher.

It is true, of course, that serious music study demands long, hard work; there is no sugar-coated path to musicianship. As children grow older and begin to have an adequate understanding of what they are working for—even though they do not always feel like practicing (and who does?)—they will realize that there are satisfactions to the hurdles they have to jump. When, however, children are too young to look beyond the present and can have no possible understanding of a goal in the minds of adults, the method of training for training's sake becomes the surest way of antagonizing the child and making him lose interest. An intelligent teacher knows this but often has to set aside her better judgment or lose her pupil. She is constantly on the lookout for opportunities to encourage technique, but she will not stress these at the expense of interest. Has she no plan, then? She most certainly has a plan—a large plan that includes both child and music, a plan that demands the best possible all-round development of that child *through* music.

Not so long ago Egon Petri, Dutch pianist and teacher, gave a piano lesson to seventeen hundred persons in Carnegie Hall. Among other things he discussed the value of practicing. "If," said he, "you work very intelligently, you don't have to work so hard as if you do it stupidly. . . . Mechanical keeping at the piano for hours and hours—that's old-fashioned.

Repetition in itself doesn't help, unless you are always experimenting." He also insisted that there is no one way to play, but that "pianists should play in the manner that is easiest and most natural." "Work intelligently" and "always experimenting"—these are exactly what we want for little children, and they will do both if given half a chance.

We must be on guard against foolproof systems of teaching music. They are many and ingenious, and each carries the guarantee that *it* is the perfect system. It is logical . . . it is painless . . . it will amuse the child. Perhaps the most dangerous of these appeals is that of being "logical." Here, we are told, is a neatly worked-out plan that leads deliberately from one stage to another; it is infallible! . . . To be sure, some teachers seem to be successful with these systems, but what is probably true is that the children learn in spite of them, for youngsters do have a way of weeding out nonessentials.

In learning to read music there is no one way that will fit all children, any more than there is in learning to read words. The secret of any teaching lies in timing it to the readiness of the child and making it fit his interest. To do this the teacher must lend himself to the child, must get under his skin, must see things his way, and above all have that rare ability to feel his way. More often than not children are ahead of us. We have grown so accustomed to thinking in terms of age levels, or are so dependent on what some authority says, that we have lost faith in our own observations and intuitions.

These suggestions of ways in which music development may occur are not to be regarded as a series of things to be taught. They are to be regarded only as possibilities. Not all children will respond to all of them, and some children may go much farther. No age level for specific experiences is indicated, for there is none. Our sensitivity to children and our knowledge of music must be our guide.

SUGGESTED BEGINNING PIANO BOOKS

Raymond Burrows, ed. *The Horace Mann Piano Book*. Boston Music Co.

Raymond Burrows and Ella Ahearn. *The Young Explorer at the Piano*. Willis Music Co.

——*Young America at the Piano*. Willis Music Co.

Floy Adele Rossman. *Keyboard Speech*. Birchard

Ernest Schelling, Charles Haak, Gail Martin and Osbourne McConathy. *Singing and Playing* (primer in the Oxford Piano Course). Oxford

4

SINGING

Burl Ives, the well-known ballad singer, was asked one day to tell how he learned to sing. "I started singing about as soon as I could talk. It was just something that went on in our family," said Ives simply. Folks were poor where he came from, but they were singing folks, and it wasn't possible for a youngster to grow up without singing too. This way of life was as natural and as necessary to his people as were eating and sleeping. And when children anywhere are happy and satisfied youngsters it is natural for them to sing, but they are indeed lucky if they live in a family where singing is something that goes on day after day.

Many people, however, are seriously concerned about the kind of songs that are right for children, and in their uncertainty they tend to underestimate their own singing repertory. There are, of course, some songs that have a particular appeal and are every child's rightful heritage. But, if there is one thing that some of us have learned with respect to choice of songs, it is this: you can't be too sure in advance what a child will or will not like!

Music cuts through all age levels. In this field there is, thank goodness, no such thing as a "chronological age." If we sing the songs that have pleasant associations for us—be they folk, popular, classical, ballad, hymn, service, or college—we shall soon discover our children's favorites. Our first concern should be to have confidence in our own musical competence, limited though it may be, and then to broaden our interests in every way we can.

FOLK SONGS. The present rebirth, for example, of our own folk-song literature offers a rich and well-nigh unlimited field for exploration. These songs are heard over the radio, on phonograph recordings, and in the theater, and many fine collections are available in book form. The bewitching melodies of *On Top of Old Smoky, Sweet Betsey from Pike, Way Down Yonder in the Pawpaw Patch,* and *Skip to My Lou,* the many beautiful Negro spirituals, and countless others have an irresistible appeal. These are songs that sing themselves, and they are loved by young and old.

CAROLS AND SONGS IN OTHER LANGUAGES. Our Christmas carols are another group of songs that stay with us—year in and year out; indeed, for many children they are year-round songs. To such children there seems nothing incongruous in singing *Silent Night* in midsummer. These carols belong to all, regardless of race, color, or creed. "Carol," by the way, originally meant a kind of dance, and "to carol" meant to dance in a joyous manner. In days long ago Christmas carols were exclusively associated with the village or community celebration of the birth of Jesus. It was a day of festivity and gayety, and it was not until much later that the Church recognized the value of the carol as a part of religious worship.

The First Nowell; Adeste, Fideles; Good King Wenceslas; Bring a Torch, Jeannette, Isabella; and *God Rest You Merry,*

Gentlemen are only a few of the more familiar ones. And for those of us who feel the urge to go exploring further, there is a wealth of carol folklore that is only beginning to come to light. One or two new collections of these less-known carols usually turn up each year at Christmas time. Occasionally we run across an edition of carols in the original languages, while some collections give both the English and the foreign versions. And if we can sing them in the original language, so much the better, for is there any happier way of becoming familiar with a foreign language than through the language of song? A little child will enjoy the "sound" of unfamiliar words, and if it is a song that has "stuck," its sounds slip naturally and easily into place and are a part of its rhythm and flow.

Songs like *Sur le pont d'Avignon; Frère Jacques; Ach, du lieber Augustin;* and *Il était une bergère* jump right across our adult barrier of literal-mindedness and find an immediate response in the sound-loving and sound-making propensities of children. If we are not at home in any language but our own, we should explore our immediate friends, neighborhood, and community. The ability to speak other languages than English is frequently overlooked by those teaching in sections where parents or grandparents are foreign-born. Naturally the school is primarily concerned with helping children in the correct use of our own language, but if we consistently overlook the cultural significance of these broader contacts in children's lives, we are missing out not only on a wonderful educational opportunity, but even more on the human-relations value of promoting better understanding among peoples.

The Scandinavian countries, Russia, Italy, Spain, France, Germany, and China, as well as our English-speaking countries across the ocean and our South American neighbors, all have their favorite and significant songs. If by good fortune we or some of our friends can bring to our children some of this musical literature, their lives will be made that much richer.

A number of folk songs have been translated and are widely used in school song books and in collections for children. In many cases the translator has caught not only the meaning of the original but also its spirit and poetic quality. In too many others, however, we find awkward and forced renderings in which not only do the words not fit the musical line, but also there is none of that feeling for the phrase which in the original made for beauty and life.

Several editors of music collections, recognizing the musical value of the folk tune, have broken away completely from the words and sense of the original song and have set new words to the melody. When this is done skillfully and with genuine regard for the relation of the content to the mood of the music, the results are gratifying. An example is *Christmas Eve,* by Mary Smith,[1] set to an old Swedish folk melody. But it can only be confusing when new words of completely different content are printed along with the original verses, for to the uninitiated it suggests that the English words are a "translation."

PATRIOTIC SONGS. Children are very sensitive to the associations built up around songs, and this is especially true of our patriotic songs. Long before he can understand the full meaning of the words of *The Star-Spangled Banner,* the youngster feels himself a living part of its spirit, and will join in lustily but with great dignity when it is sung. Certainly this is a difficult song to sing, not only for children but for most adults, but

[1] Glenn, Leavitt, and Rebemann. *Sing a Song* (The World of Music Series). Ginn.

the child's inability to stay on tune and to reach its "musical top" are far outweighed by the profound feelings called forth by his experience. *Anchors Aweigh, The Marines' Hymn, When Johnny Comes Marching Home, The Battle Hymn of the Republic, Yankee Doodle,* and many other songs of this character all have a way of helping to make a child feel a part of a larger world.

COMMUNITY SONGS. It is impossible, naturally, to list all the songs that belong to our various backgrounds, but some are known and loved by singing Americans the country over. Among these are songs associated with happy times when folks get together, such as *Sweet Adeline; My Bonnie Lies over the Ocean; Goodnight, Ladies; Reuben and Rachel; K-K-K-Katy; Row, Row, Row Your Boat; Oh, No, John; Loch Lomond; Home on the Range,* Stephen Foster's songs, and Negro spirituals. Most of these are easy to sing and the child picks them up quickly. He is likely also to become familiar with snatches from the popular tunes of the day. All is grist that comes to his mill.

How does a child respond to these songs? It depends on the song, on the way in which it comes to him, and on the child himself. In some cases he will be content merely to listen, but what an active listener he can be! At other times he will sing only parts of a song. A refrain or chorus in which there is repetition of words and melody will be his in no time. For example, he can immediately tune in on and be a part of a song where there is repetition of syllables such as Fa la la la, la —la la la, la, la, in *Deck the Halls with Boughs of Holly,* and in the English narrative folk song, *There Was an Old Woman as I've Heard Tell.* Many of these songs, especially the folk songs, are easy to sing, and the child can soon sing the entire song. Botkin defines folklore as the "stuff that travels and the stuff that sticks." [2] Folk songs stick because of their simplicity of form, their singability, and their genuineness.

So far this chapter has been concerned with urging all of us who live with children to make every effort to detect and use our musical powers; otherwise we have no solid foundation on which to build. The voice is an instrument that we have with us always, but unfortunately, in these days of ready-made music, many have forgotten how to use it. Great artists come to our homes over the radio and through phonograph recordings, and in our enjoyment of their talent it is very easy to lose touch with our own musical selves. But these very inventions can, and in many homes do, stimulate the making of music by every member of the family even to the canary! The chances are that all of us have much more familiarity with music tucked away in our past than we have any idea of, and spreading our musical interests will frequently mean tapping these long-forgotten associations.

CHILDREN'S SONGS. There are many songs that belong especially to childhood; lacking these, a child's musical life is a lean one. Creative songs that he makes up about himself and the things that go on in his world; songs that others, inspired by his improvisations, have written for him; imaginative and realistic songs both contemporary and traditional—all of these offer rich singing experiences and lasting enjoyment.

The younger the child, the more free and unconventional his singing talk is likely to be; but as he grows older and is exposed more and more to music around him, he begins to be conditioned by its form and tonality, and, in turn, his creative expressions show this influence.

[2] Ben Botkin. *A Treasury of American Folklore*. Crown.

MAKE-UP SONGS. A great deal has been talked and written about the child's creative songs, and a number of songs illustrating his free and spontaneous expression have been recorded. Some of these first songs have a charm and freshness all their own, but their importance lies not so much in their intrinsic musical value as in what happens to the child as he sings them. We may choose to record a few of them quietly and unobtrusively, or help the child to find them on an instrument, and then sing or play them back to him. If this procedure serves to stimulate him to more music-making, well and good; but if, as happens many times, the adult takes to refining and polishing the product, or if the child becomes unduly conscious of his own genius and basks in the reflected glory of his creation, it is obvious that it is not only his musical development that suffers!

It is important that these beginnings of music making should focus on the constant encouragement of this *way of expressing himself* and not on the product itself. As the child grows older and is consciously interested in composing songs and having someone record them for him, and even learning how to record them himself, he becomes more aware of his ability to create. If, however, this stage of development (which belongs to a later period) is forced on him prematurely, he is likely in his preoccupation with the symbols of music to miss the core of the art that the symbols represent. What is important is not the preservation of any special song that a child creates, but the preservation of a way of life that will keep on inspiring him to experiment freely.

EXPERIENCE SONGS. One way of encouraging and supplementing the child's early efforts at song-making is to bring to him

The more informal times for singing that a parent or a teacher can arrange, the better

They can do anything! "Swimming," somersaulting, doing tricks on the floor are not only natural expressions of a child's exuberance, but recognized as important by dance teachers

some of the songs that have been written about him and his world—songs about swinging, running, and jumping, songs about dressing and undressing, songs about animals, about boats, trains, and airplanes, and simple festival songs.

A few collections of this type of song have lovely colored illustrations that appeal to little children and that help to stimulate their interest in singing. Children like to have someone sit down with them and sing through a book, repeating over and over again their special favorites. Many of these songs are arranged so that the child's own name or his particular interest can be sung about; the song merely provides the framework for his personal experiences. Moreover, little children are just as likely to be stimulated to singing by any favorite picture book as by a song book; to them the absence of music makes no difference.

The more frequent the periods for informal singing a parent or teacher can have with little children, the better. It would be unfortunate if we felt that we always had to play the piano to accompany a song. Children use song in a functional way, just as folk music was originally used.

SONGS OF THE SEASONS. Songs about the seasons of the year have always been sung, and here again folk music gives us some of our most delightful melodies; *The North Wind Doth Blow, Tirra, Lirra, Lirra,* and *All the Birds Have Come Again* are examples. The younger children are fond of such songs as *Swish, Swish Go the Leaves*[3] and *The Weather Is Warm.*[4] And was ever a song more beloved by young and old than *Jingle Bells?*

[3] *Seasons and Such* by Leyden. Grosset.

[4] *Another Singing Time* by Satis Coleman and Alice G. Thorn. John Day.

HOLIDAYS. Holidays, too, come in for their share of celebration in song. Tradition plays a great part, especially in relation to such a holiday as Christmas. The most personal of all holidays to a child is his birthday, and no birthday is complete without *Happy Birthday to You.* Hallowe'en is celebrated by songs about Jack o' Lanterns, pumpkins, and witches; Easter, by songs about bunnies and Easter eggs.

Then we have the patriotic holidays such as Independence Day and the birthdays of Washington and Lincoln. There was a time when teachers felt that special songs must accompany all these occasions, and as a result songs were "manufactured" by the music companies to fill this need. Almost without exception such songs are forced and artificial, and have no value musically. Little children find these holidays of no more than passing interest, and they should be made conscious of them in a more natural way and with a frank recognition of the limitations of their interest.

LULLABIES. Lullabies, the first songs a mother sings to her baby, are in turn sung by small girls to their dollies. We should not want any child to grow up without being at home with *Rockabye, Baby; Sleep, Baby, Sleep;* Brahms's *Cradle Song; Go to Sleep, Pierrot, Little Brother;* and *Away in a Manger.* Each country has its own lullabies, and if our children can hear some of these in the original languages their musical experiences will be by so much the richer.

HUMOROUS SONGS. While it is, of course, not possible to touch upon every kind of song enjoyed by children, one type certainly must not be left out: the humorous song. There are far too few of these, and even these few are not brought to children often enough. The pure nonsense song is enjoyed tremendously, providing a welcome outlet for a youngster's love of fun.

Some funny songs, like *This Old Man* and *Willy, Willy, Will,* depend for their humor upon an infectious repetition of syllables. Others, like *Aiken Drum, Polly Wolly Doodle, The Bear Went over the Mountain,* and *The Gingerbread Lady,* appeal largely because of their ridiculous content. These are songs that the whole family can enjoy together.

SINGING GAMES. When we observe a group of little children playing *The Farmer in the Dell, London Bridge, Little Sally Waters,* or any other familiar and simply organized game, we are almost certain to see every member of the group singing. Even a child who is not likely to sing easily at other times will lose himself in the game and sing. This is a truly functional experience, for singing is needed to keep the game going. Then, too, the character of the music and the words of the song make it very easy for him to do his part. A great deal of repetition both in words and music makes these songs easy to sing and hard to forget.

Little children learn many game songs long before they are able to participate in a group game. They hear older boys and girls singing them in their play, and a few of them are usually included in collections of traditional songs for children. Edna Potter has compiled and illustrated a collection of singing games.[5] Little children will enjoy this beautiful book as a picture song book, or will occasionally "play out" a song in their own way. For example, a four-year-old asked to play *The Muffin Man,* and it developed that her idea was to have all the girls, holding their skirts straight out in front with both hands, stand at one end of the room, and all the boys stand at

[5] Edna Potter. *This Way and That.* Oxford.

the other end. She asked the adult to sing the song, and then the boys were told to walk over and take muffins out of the little girls' skirts!

This simplification of a game is a perfectly satisfactory way of playing for the younger children. In *London Bridge,* for example, passing through under the bridge and singing the song are much more fun than standing behind the bridge-holders after having been caught. Children use this song in many ways. A small group of five-year-olds playing on a see-saw had a hilarious time improvising on the verse "Build it up with iron bars." Nothing was too ridiculous to fit into this framework: "Build it up with bacon and eggs"—"with shoes and stockings"—"with toads and mice"—and so on.

In any group there is likely to be one "conformist" (we hope it won't be the grown-up) who insists on following the rules of the game. If the adult with the group feels that the traditional organization of this particular game is beyond the children's social development, it is well to direct their play to a simpler form, saying that there are different ways of playing games just as there are different ways of singing the song. Here is an excellent opportunity to tell children how folk songs have come down to us and why it is that the same song may have several variations.

ROUNDS. Singing rounds is a musical experience usually associated with older children and adults. It has been our experience, however, that while little children cannot carry on alone the organization of round-singing, the five- and six-year-olds greatly enjoy being a part of this type of group singing. If there are two grown-ups with a group, the children can be divided and can follow their leaders in a two-part round. One of our kindergarten Christmas celebrations was remembered especially by the children because the visiting parents and friends joined the children in singing *Frère Jacques* in round form. This was so much fun that long before Lincoln's Birthday the children planned to ask their fathers (who were to visit the school on that day) to sing *Row, Row, Row Your Boat* with them.

STANDARDS FOR CHOOSING SONGS. By analyzing the characteristics of the various types of songs discussed above, we shall arrive at a good basis for judgment on the choice of new songs written especially for children. For while there is great value in the song that has stood the test of time, we must also be on the alert for fresh contributions to the field.

First of all, a song must be good musically: that is, it must have a lovely melody, one that is easy to sing yet unhackneyed. We are all well aware of the popular tune that takes us by storm but after a month or two dies a natural death. Only a skilled critic can tell why a few of our contemporary songs live, and why most of them are soon forgotten.

The rhythmic flow of a song is also important. Is there sufficient repetition of both rhythmic and melodic pattern as well as of content idea to make it a song that is easily learned and remembered?

The music of a song is of more importance than the words. The content, nevertheless, should express a genuine emotion and in a childlike way. The best songs come from real experience. There was a time when songs written for children were full of rosebud babies and personified seasons! These songs have long been forgotten because they did not reflect children's real interests.

Not long ago a radio singer whose programs for children had become very popular attributed part of his success to the fact that he had transposed many of the children's songs he sang to a key lower than that in which they were written. On his program he encouraged children who were listening in at home to sing along with him, and he knew that many songs written for them are beyond the comfortable range of the average child's voice.

In the last analysis, children are our best natural critics. If they live in a rich musical environment they acquire an almost uncanny ability to sort out the good from the poor. They may go overboard occasionally for an insignificant song, but in the long run their taste is reliable.

CHILD VOICE. The "high, sweet voice" so often attributed to little children is a myth so far as most youngsters are concerned. The average range of tones is from around middle C to C or D above. For the nursery-age child, songs within five tones or even three are more easily learned than those that have a wider range. Naturally, a child should hear more than these songs, but if his singing voice is to be encouraged he should be exposed to many songs that are easy for him.

Jersild and Bienstock report [6] that while children sing more easily when a song is changed to a lower pitch, they tend to use higher tones in the spontaneous use of their voices. This study emphasized the importance of helping children discover their singing potentiality at least by the end of the third grade; otherwise there is a danger of their falling into the habit of not using their singing voices—a habit difficult to compensate later.

When it comes to singing ability, some people are just born lucky, having a keen sensitivity to pitch plus a natural ability

[6] "A Study of the Development of Children's Ability to Sing." *Journal of Educational Psychology,* October 1934.

to sing easily and accurately. At the opposite end of the pole are the persons called "tone deaf." It has been estimated that in any given group one child may be two hundred times as sensitive to pitch as another. This by no means implies that every person is aware of his full potentiality; intelligent training can be of inestimable value if it is directed to the full exploration of that potentiality.

It is unfortunate that children who use a limited range of their voices are often called "monotones." There *may* be real monotones, though in our experience with many children over a period of years we have not encountered a single one. True, some children's singing voices tend toward monotony, lacking flexibility; usually their speaking voices show the same tendency, lacking inflection. If we have sharp ears we can notice that these same children frequently use a different register of their voices during spontaneous play; in other words, the motivation of the play spirit calls forth from the child a higher pitch of his voice than any singing experience would do. We have found it helpful to utilize, *at the time it happens,* this type of experience—not in a formal way, so that the child is conscious of the fact, but by joining in his play. (See Chapter 1.) High places usually stimulate the use of the higher register of the voice.

It is not, then, specific vocal training that will encourage a little child to find "different places" in his voice so much as the way in which we encourage him to play with his voice and gradually help him be aware of its possibilities. What these children need most of all is to be helped to get a "spring" in their voices, to be encouraged in the sheer manipulation of sound. They should at the same time get acquainted with many songs that are easy for them to sing. There is nothing quite so frustrating to anyone, young or old, as to be constantly confronted with experiences in which they cannot achieve conscious success.

Another characteristic of children's singing that we must be prepared for is that it is more vigorous than exact. There are times—many times—when a youngster feels like giving all he has, and that can be a great deal! He is full of robust feelings, and the sweet, light voice so often demanded by singing teachers in no way measures up to these feelings. Children's moods, however, are not always dynamic. If they have a legitimate amount of outlet for their strong feelings, they will tend toward a balance, so that there will be many times when they find it natural to sing less vigorously. It is our job to see that they have music to fit all their moods, and to recognize the importance of balance in their experiences.

SKILLS IN SINGING. All through this chapter on singing, we have tried to keep in the reader's mind not only the characteristics of children's singing but also the ways in which we can help children to a better use of their voices. We believe that skills in the use of the voice are developed in the many informal day-by-day experiences rather than in specific training.

What then of the techniques that have been the music supervisor's standby in training the child's voice? For example, is there no place for the tone drill (matching tones of another voice or of an instrument), the echo game, the pass word, the singing names, the question-and-answer, and other drills?

If we are observant, we can find the roots of practically all these techniques in the daily play of little children. Not that it is wise to utilize every opportunity, but there are many times when a child will welcome this variation of his play so long as the adult is careful that it does not become forced or artificial. Occasionally with older children some of these games can be carried over to a "music time." If the child welcomes this, well and good; but if he becomes self-conscious, the procedure defeats its purpose.

In our concern for developing skills we must always keep in mind the following:

Love of singing is of first importance;

Specific training should be used only if we have the child's interest and co-operation;

Be careful to differentiate between improvement and accuracy;

Do not resort to competition in order to raise standards;

Encourage children to listen to their own voices and to the voices of others.[7]

TEACHING SONGS. The most effective teaching of songs occurs when the song fits the mood of the children. This does not mean that every activity a child engages in must have a song experience related to it. Though a song about a train may sometimes be just what a child will welcome if he is engaged in building a train, this is not invariably true. Music is not of the intellect, and a sensitive person will feel the mood of a child in bringing him a sensory experience.

If we can sing accurately without the use of an instrument, so much the better. But if we are not too sure of ourselves, it is better to play the melody on an instrument and sing along with it. There are many times, too, when the child will enjoy not only the melody but also the accompaniment played on the piano, provided the playing is well done and supports but does not drown out the voice. Naturally, if we must depend on a piano to accompany us, we shall miss many opportunities

[7] Conscious listening to such instruments as flute or violin seldom fails to give a lift to children's voices.

to sing songs. The adult, moreover, must *know* the song, and must present it free of mannerisms and dramatic affectations; what is required is good enunciation and simple directness together with a pleasant quality of tone.

Songs are made to be sung, not to be talked about, and preliminary explanations and discussions are thus not only unnecessary but inartistic. The song should be sung through from beginning to end, and we must not be disturbed if children's enthusiasms urge them to join in even before they know what is coming next. *After* they have participated, they will usually be willing to listen to the song several times without trying to sing it.

Wherever the child is, at home or at school, his environment must be free of tensions and conflicts. Pleasant, "easy" surroundings are an absolute requisite if we wish a child to develop an interest in and love for singing. And if all of us who are interested in children's musical development concern ourselves less with "the teaching of singing" and more with seeing to it that singing is something that goes on in our family or in our school, the results—the kind of results that really count—will bob up of their own accord.

SONGS FOR CHILDREN

Inez Bertail (ed.), Masha (illus.). *A Child's Book of Christmas Carols.* Random House. Charming illustrations of familiar carols.

Satis Coleman and Alice G. Thorn. *The Little Singing Time.* John Day. A music picture book for the very little child.

Satis Coleman and Alice G. Thorn. *Singing Time.* John Day. Illustrated songs about children's interests.

——*Another Singing Time.* John Day. More songs about children and their interests.

Dorothy B. Commins. *Lullabies of Many Lands.* Harper. An unusual collection of lullabies.

Pelagie Doan (illus.). *Favorite Nursery Songs.* Random House. Gay illustrations for old favorites.

Leah Gale (arranged by), Corinne Malvern (illus.). *Nursery Songs.* Simon & Schuster.

Mabelle Glenn, Helen Leavitt, and Victor Rebmann. *Sing a Song.* Ginn. A collection of songs to fit every occasion—many folk tunes.

Mary Nancy Graham (compiler). *Christmas Carols.* Whitman. Illustrated collection of familiar carols.

——*Fifty Favorite Songs for Boys and Girls.* Whitman. Familiar nursery and folk songs.

Heribert and Johannes Gruger. *The Sing Song Picture Book.* J. B. Lippincott.

Berta and Elmer Hader. *A Picture Book of Mother Goose.* Coward-McCann. Beautifully illustrated and a great favorite.

Evelyn Hunt. *Music Time.* Viking. Experience songs.

Clara Lyden. *Children, Come and Sing.* Grosset. Songs about the seasons for the very young.

Laura P. MacCartney. *Songs for the Nursery School.* Willis. Short, simple songs for the youngest as well as a large group for the older child. Songs about transportation, animals, parades and other things of interest to children.

Edna Potter. *This Way and That.* Oxford. A book of twenty-four singing games, all great favorites. Attractively illustrated.

Julius Röntgen. *Old Dutch Nursery Rhymes.* [English version by R. H. Elkin] McKay. Beautifully illustrated by Willebeek Le Mair.

Karl Schulte (ed.), Miss Elliott (illus.). *Favorite Hymns for Children.* Grosset.

Ruth Crawford Seeger. *American Folk Songs for Children.* Doubleday. Outstanding collection and highly recommended.

Gustaf Tenggren (illus.). *New Illustrated Book of Favorite Hymns.* Garden City.

Katharine Tyler Wessels (selected by), Gertrude Elliott (illus.). *The Golden Song Book.* Simon & Schuster. Excellent collection of sixty favorite songs and singing games.

Opal Wheeler (selected by), Tenggren (illus.). *Sing for America.* Dutton. Stories, pictures, and music of favorite songs.

SONG COLLECTIONS FOR THE FAMILY

Margaret Bradford Boni. *Fireside Book of Folk Songs.* Simon & Schuster.

Satis Coleman and Elin K. Jörgensen. *Christmas Carols from Many Countries.* Schirmer. A large collection of familiar carols and many others not so familiar. Original language and translations.

Percy Dearmer, R. Vaughan Williams, and Martin Shaw. *Oxford Book of Carols.* Oxford. A classic collection of carols.

Margaret and Travis Johnson. *Early American Songs.* Associated Music Publishers.

Sylvia and John Kolb. *A Treasury of Folk Songs.* Bantam.

Harry Robert Wilson. *Songs of the Hills and Plains.* Hall & McCreary.

SOURCE BOOKS OF AMERICAN SONGS AND THEIR HISTORY

Ben Botkin. *A Treasury of American Folklore*. Crown.
Frank Luther. *Americans and their Songs*. Harper.
John A. and Alan Lomax. *American Ballads and Folk Songs*. Macmillan.
—— *Our Singing Country*. Macmillan.
Carl Sandburg. *American Song Bag*. Harcourt.
Dorothy Scarborough. *A Song Catcher in Southern Mountains*. Colorado University Press.
Frank Shay. *American Sea Songs and Chanteys*. North.
Jean Thomas. *Ballad Makin' in the Mountains of Kentucky*. Holt.

SOURCE BOOKS OF CHILDREN'S RHYMES AND GAMES

Marion Vallat Emrich and George Korson. *The Child's Book of Folklore*. Dial.
Ione and Peter Opie (eds.). *The Oxford Dictionary of Nursery Rhymes*. Oxford. Comprehensive collection of traditional rhymes and songs and their individual histories.
Marion Webb. *Games for Younger Children*. Morrow.
Carl Withers. *A Rocket in My Pocket*. Holt. A unique collection of children's rhymes taken directly from their street play. Full of rhythm and word play.

5

DANCE

As CHILDREN APPROACH MUSIC through their interest in sound and rhythm, so they approach dance through their instinctive interest in movement. They are full of animal spirits: running and jumping, rolling and crawling, pushing and pulling, and, with leaps and bounds, they are all over the place. To Mother and Dad, life seems to be just one catapult after another! Unhappy indeed is the home that does not provide unencumbered space for Junior—and unhappy is Junior if the avoidance of precious antiques and knickknacks calls for too much self-control.

"To prevent bodily weakness and infirmity, exercise is necessary: and one physician has said that he did not know what was most necessary to the human frame, *food* or *motion*." Over one hundred and forty years have passed since this statement appeared in *Youthful Recreation,* a magazine published in Philadelphia. It would be interesting to know what this physician meant by "motion." Was he thinking of some prescribed form of exercise, or of games, or of the usual normal activity of daily life? The demands of our early farm and village life went a long way toward satisfying the needs of physical development that in modern life have to be artificially provided for. Whether or not our forefathers were conscious of the importance of "motion," it was of necessity a part of their very existence.

In recent years, through our study of the nature of the child and how he grows, we have learned a great deal about the value of physical activity. Specialists in the field of child development have told us what children need, and manufacturers have produced a large variety of equipment to satisfy these needs. The home and the school have become increasingly conscious of the necessity of providing adequately for children's physical development. The slide has taken the place of the cellar door; the jungle gym, of trees. We have parks and playgrounds equipped with apparatus, and we see to it that children have an opportunity to use this equipment.

Too often, however, we think that when we have supplied certain equipment, we have taken care of all the child's exercising needs, and we are prone not only to overlook the value of his use of movement unrelated to equipment, but even to discourage it. Mothers, in their desire for cleanliness, urge their babies to walk rather than creep, or keep them confined to a small place until they are able to walk. Yet physical-growth specialists tell us that children stop creeping too soon, and nursery schools encourage this way of moving about by providing low places to crawl through and under. With most children this is a natural movement unless it is denied them.

Schools are at fault as much as homes; building superintendents and administrators accept the fact that children in the nursery school use the floors, but kindergarten and primary teachers have a constant struggle (usually a losing one) with the powers that be to have the floors kept clean enough so that older children may use them freely. Make no mistake about it: the fun of tumbling, rolling, and sliding does not belong exclusively to a nursery-school curriculum. If we watch any group of four-, five-, or six-year-olds (and even older) we shall find that a large part of their time is spent on the floor, either in such activities as block building or just in the sheer physical enjoyment of tumbling all around.

Healthy children are active because they are made that way. The inner demand that they feel for movement is as strong as the need they feel for food. Their muscles and their whole bodies cry out to be used, and use them they must—or not only they, but those who live with them, will know the consequences!

In the world of movement, then, as in the world of sound, we have the children's enthusiasm and wholehearted interest, to say nothing of their amazing ability in the use of their bodies. Since the dance is built on movement, children from the very beginning are at home in the elements of that art which, according to John Martin,[1] is the most fundamental of all arts.

Dance is essentially a creative medium in itself—not merely an interpretation of music. We must comprehend fully the meaning of this, for here, as in other fields, it is easy to give lip service to a fundamental principle, and in practice to follow our traditional ways. In our schools, the teaching of music and rhythms has been deeply rooted in tradition. We talk a great deal about creative dance, or (in nursery schools and kindergartens) about creative rhythms; but with younger children, at least, we have tied it up so closely with music that no real creativeness is possible.[2]

[1] John Martin. *Modern Dance*. Barnes.

[2] In this discussion we are not concerned with the traditional dances, such as folk and ballet, since these serve a different purpose in that they carry on from one generation to another cultural and traditional dance forms. They are the result of specialized training, and are obviously not suited to the stage of development of young children.

Perhaps if we compare the art of movement with another art—painting, for example—we can see more clearly how we have unintentionally handicapped children in their use of movement as it relates to the dance. When we give paints to a child, we do not tell him what to paint—we encourage him to use his own initiative in experimenting with color and line. His first interest is in the art material itself and what he can do with it, and the teacher will not hurry this stage.

In movement, however, we play music for a child and ask him to listen to it and "do what it says"! In other words, we start out with a framework into which we expect the child to fit his idea. If we were to carry this method over into painting, we should say to the child: "Here are paints that you may use in painting a picture of a house." But someone will say: "Yes, we play music, but we tell the child to do what he likes to it." Carrying this analogy further, we should then say to the child who is painting: "You may paint any kind of house you wish, but you *must* paint a house"!

For when music is played for children and they are asked to move to it, a pattern and a mood are set that limit the type of movement. Or we have the situation in which music goes on, but the children do whatever they please, regardless of the accompaniment. In the first case, a child's creativeness is limited; in the second, music ceases to have any meaning as related to the movement.

One of the greatest contributions made by modern dance has been its recognition of the independence of movement as an art medium. Music is used to support it; it is part of the scenery; it is the handmaiden of the dance. Many times it is composed especially for the dance, since music that will clearly interpret the movement cannot always be found.

Those of us who work with little children have much to

learn from a study of contemporary dance if we would be understanding guides of their use of movement. We have given them opportunity for unhampered physical activity on the playground and during their free periods; but as soon as a small group come together for dancing, we have been too eager not only to tie up their ideas immediately to music but also to use music as a stimulus. We forget that children's ideas and their urge to sheer physical activity are a much more powerful and vital stimulus than any music we can offer, and a far more rewarding one if we wish to capture their enthusiasm. We must therefore give them every opportunity to use their "material"—the material of movement—and train ourselves in recognizing their natural functional movements as our most important asset in teaching.

What are the natural movements of children unrelated to music? Generally speaking, physical activity is motivated in two ways. First, there is activity for activity's sake. This is a result of exuberance of spirits, and takes a variety of forms, such as the baby's erratic movements of arms and legs, and the older child's tumbling, rolling, somersaulting, jumping, and skipping. Second, there is movement that is stimulated by ideas, in which children's imagination is the driving force, such as animal, boat, or airplane play.

In a child's spontaneous play we have a wonderful opportunity to observe his individual movements and to utilize these. What we do with them depends on ability to sense his readiness for help. Perhaps seeing to it that he has free space in which to experiment will be all the help he needs; perhaps he will welcome someone to play with him and thus add encouragement to his play; perhaps he will be ready for an extension of his play by having another see more possibilities in it; perhaps his movement has enough of a simple rhythmic pattern to benefit by the addition of an accompaniment, or he may accompany himself by chanting or singing a song; or the adult may supply a song, or chant, or clap her hands, or use an instrument to support his play.

A child's feeling for rhythmic movement cannot be forced; it must wait on his development. If he is given space and encouragement, he will proceed at his own rate. It is also recognized that this rate will be different for each child. Frequently we hear a mother say: "My child has no rhythm—he can't keep time to music." But each child has his own rhythm, determined by such factors as his weight, height, and temperament. The rhythm of the light, dynamic child is different from that of the heavy, lethargic child. Your natural rhythm is different from mine, but we have learned to control ours at will to conform to a common pattern. In the beginning, then, it is important for us to have *our music keep time to the child* rather than ask him to conform to our time. In other words, have *music listen* to *children,* and not *children listen* to *music!*

Too many of us are overconcerned about our lack of musical skill. We, too, can use our feelings just as children do, and, if necessary, imitate their movement in order to get the "feel" of it. This rhythm can then be transferred to a simple instrument such as a tom-tom. At times, we can help to make a child conscious of his rhythm by saying: "This is how your feet sound when you go running," or "This is the way you go when you roll over and over." Catching his rhythm by clapping or tapping will make him conscious of differences much more quickly than starting out with our own distinctions between running and rolling. After many experiences of this kind, children are ready and eager to listen to our rhythms occasionally, and to follow them.

By far the larger part of little children's experiences in

rhythmic play will be individual. Sometimes, however, several of the older children in a nursery-age group will play together, and may be able to accommodate themselves to a rhythm (one set by another child or by an adult); but a group of this kind should be a flexible one, allowing individual children to come and go according to their interest. Children should be invited, but *never forced,* to come to dancing time; and, if they do come, they should be free to leave when their interest is satisfied. Individual children may show sustained interest, and with these we should go along as far as their interest carries them.

A word about the so-called "doctrine of interest" may not be amiss here, since it has recently come in for a great deal of discussion—sometimes for unfortunate misunderstanding. We hear considerable talk in nursery-school circles about "incidental" learnings. The environment is carefully planned, children live in it and learn from it, and teachers do not hesitate to step in to guide them in their social development or in routine habits. Often, however, there is found extreme reluctance on the part of the teacher to bring in new experiences in content, as an extension of the child's interest; or else there is a tendency to go to the other extreme, especially in dance and music, and impose a program that belongs to the stage of development of older children.

In the first case the adult has not fully explored the possibilities of children's interests, and in the second she has not recognized the limitations of their physical and social development. There is a vast difference between being unaware of the existence of something and having it thrust upon one. Boredom can be overstimulating, too! We must not overshoot the mark, not mistake our interest for the child's; we *should* be sure that we reach for the child's maximum possibilities rather than rest content with his minimum.

In a person who is not a trained musician, some of this hesitation springs from insecurity. She cannot play the piano, or perhaps there is no piano, and she feels that she cannot help children in music. What she needs is not skill in performance so much as skill in "feeling" and understanding. If she can rediscover in herself that curiosity in sound and movement with which children are endowed, her guidance of their musical interests may well surpass that of a concert artist.

Recently we visited a nursery school in charge of a young woman who had had no musical training. She had, however, a genuine love of music and was keenly alert to the ways in which children use movement and sound. She learned and "felt" with them, and this little group had, without exception, the richest musical environment of any group we have observed. Experiences in music and dance in this nursery school were "incidental plus"—not accidental. The children were alive to the joy of these arts, and their teacher became so interested that she lost no time in enrolling in a class in modern dance in order to learn more about movement.

Skill in an art is no handicap. Indeed, it should be a tremendous asset, since the more we know about an art, the more possibilities we see in it, and the richer experiences we can bring to children—provided we have not lost our "at-homeness" with its soul and body.

But to get back to children and their never-ending quest for action. We accept such exercise as running, jumping, and skipping as part of the growing-up process, but when it comes to activities in which the child rolls, slides, "swims," somersaults, pulls himself along over the floor, or does a hundred and one ingenious tricks with his body, we may tolerate these capers, but we seldom encourage them, at least in connection with a dance program.

Yet these large floor movements in which the child uses not only his arms and legs, but more especially his torso, are recognized by dance teachers as fundamentally important. Their contribution, too, to the development of good posture is obvious, and they undoubtedly have great therapeutic value as an outlet for children's feelings, which in turn makes for a sense of security and well-being.

The psychological importance of these primitive reactions is stressed by Bender and Boas: "The whole system of postures is fundamentally different when an individual is lying on the ground. . . . The usual dances keep the individual in the upright position. They restrict the possible varieties of postural experiences. The whole muscle tone is different when standing."[3]

These more primitive movements, being full of vigor and strength, appeal especially to boys—though boys have no priority rights in them! "Stunts" time should be a part of any dance period, and it will be if the children have anything to say about it—and if the teacher is aware of the many dance "leads" that are offered by the group through this kind of activity.

A good vigorous workout virtually massages the body, and, when it is over, the children are only too ready to "let go" and lie flat on the floor for a short rest. Full relaxation, the kind achieved by reaction from its opposite, comes through a feeling in the muscles themselves and not through any outside stimulus or device. Children are ready to rest because their bodies feel the need of change.

It is essential, especially when children live in groups, to give them the opportunity for vigorous play in order to relieve

[3] "Creative Dance in Therapy." *American Journal of Orthopsychiatry*, April 1941.

tensions. What really makes for overstimulation is the program that stresses inactivity and quietness—and obtains these by "busy work"! This holds true both in the home and at school.

In helping children to explore movement, our effectiveness will depend on how much we know about its possibilities, and nothing will contribute so much to that knowledge as our own personal participation. We shall also add to it by attending dance concerts, for two reasons: a dance concert is a vicarious experience if we approach it with our kinesthetic sense and not with our intellect; and we cannot help comparing many of the artists' dance movements with the way in which children use their bodies.

If children seem to be limited in their experimentation (though they seldom are), they can sometimes be helped to explore other possibilities by such suggestions as the following: "How many ways can you find to cross the room without using your feet?" They will usually discover an infinite variety of ways! "See what you can do when you are lying on your back." Occasionally they will enjoy isolating certain parts of their bodies, using (for example) only their fingers, or arms, or head, or legs, or "middles"!

To children, "stunts" are much of the time just stunts, without any association of dramatic ideas; again, imagination may enter in, or it may even be the motivating force. For example, two five-year-olds were each walking on "all fours" with their faces towards the ceiling. One was a dinosaur and the other was a walking table! As the walking table was an especially good idea, it was not long before the room was full of walking tables—with "chairs" under some of them. This was a fine game and—after several days of it—in order to supplement it we accompanied the walking chairs and tables by reciting *The Table and the Chair* by Edward Lear.

One day a four-year-old all curled up into a huddle propelled himself across the playground with an irregular bumping movement, telling us that he was a cake of ice running away from the iceman. "Snakes," another favorite dramatization, requires a good deal of active wriggling of the torso.

All children play airplanes, trains, and boats. Here again, such activities are accepted at face value during free play, but in a dancing group the teacher hesitates to work from the idea itself, and instead immediately plays (for example) airplane music, usually getting so busy with reading and playing the music that she loses sight of the children! "The dance is more nearly related to drama than to music. This one exception is that of time—rhythm. Dance and drama are internally related! They are of the same essential stuff; one works in the medium of movement, the other of action which are practically inseparable. The dance and music are only externally related to the extent that both make formal patterns in the one common dimension of time." [4]

The natural accompaniment of airplanes—for the young child, at least—is the rhythm of his own motor, and we do not need sharp ears to hear its rhythmic flow. The sustained sound of the child's accompaniment fits the uninterrupted rhythmic movement of the airplane much better than any piano accompaniment can do.

This type of dramatic play should be developed in the directions of bringing in added content (usually the children know more about airplanes than their elders do!), of discussions, and of helping the children to become aware of the motor's rhythm and its natural rise and fall in intensity. There may be times when a piano can be used advantageously, but in our experi-

[4] John Martin. *The Modern Dance.* Barnes.

ence the piano has usually reduced the emotional tone of the play.

The traditional way of playing trains is another example of how our preconceptions can handicap the child's use of an idea. One morning while a few children were sitting on the floor waiting for the rest of the group to change their shoes, they began to shuffle their feet back and forth because they liked the sound of their chamois dancing shoes on the floor. Almost at once the shuffling took on a definite rhythmic pattern. Soon the children were accompanying these "trains" by saying *choo-choo,* and we supported their rhythm by slapping a large drum with one hand and swishing back and forth over a second drum with the other hand.

These trains, however, were not active enough to keep their attention for long. One child wanted to play train in the good old-fashioned way, and of course *she* wanted to be the engine. But so did twenty-five others! Obviously, taking turns would not solve this problem, because there would be too many turns! Since engines are the most dramatic part of trains to youngsters, we suggested that each one be an engine, and then he could haul any kind of train that pleased him. The engines took various forms—some shuffling ahead on their feet, some moving on all fours, some sitting down and shoving along; one child, swinging one arm in a wide, revolving movement, showed that it was the engine wheels that loomed largest in his experience.

In connection with little children's dramatic play, it is important to remember that they are not interested in "composing" a train, for example, according to any picture we may have in our mind. They seize upon what is to them the most outstanding aspect of an idea, and they dramatize that. Nor is this a mere process of "imitation." They jump right into the heart of the idea. They are not like an engine: they *are* an engine!

As children grow older, they become more interested in the picture of the whole, and themselves take the initiative in planning for its various parts and in choosing each other to dramatize these parts. Unfortunately, this later stage of development is too often thrust upon younger children by an unimaginative adult who wants to see results as *she* pictures them. But when we are able to retain the children's enthusiasm by utilizing their ideas, and helping them develop these ideas along the lines of their own thinking, we get results that are vital and truly creative.

It is obvious from the foregoing examples that accompaniment must be flexible if we wish to work from movement rather than from music. Accompaniment can give the child's experience greater meaning and perhaps extend it, but *flexibility* in *thinking* on the part of all concerned is an absolute essential underlying the whole process. What type of music, or what kind of sound, or what sound-making instrument will best heighten this particular idea?

Moreover, the accompanist will not only have to be flexible in her choice of sound; often she will also have to improvise. Yet even the untrained musician need not feel discouraged, since there are many possibilities for the amateur in such percussion instruments as drums and gongs and temple bells. These offer a variety of sounds and lend themselves as well to the grown-up's experimental impulses as to the child's. A child, too, can easily learn to accompany the movement of another child; and, in a group, much valuable experience can be gained by having several children work independently while the teacher is busy with other things.

The large gong is a very dramatic instrument whose climactic effect thrills the children. To be used to best advantage it should be suspended from a stand. And they should make acquaintance with it out of doors, first, rather than indoors, for it is capable of giving out "big" sounds, and children's early experimentation is none too controlled! When played in a steady, low tremolo, it will induce relaxation. It can be used to great advantage also in accompanying a sustained, flowing movement.

All too frequently we fail to realize how important climaxes are to children, and in working with a group we do everything possible to avoid these lest the group get out of control. But children who are given a chance to "explode" once in a while are much less likely to get out of hand than they are if the lid is kept clamped on tight. How often we have seen a child running faster and faster, "louder and louder," working up to an intensity that reaches its climax with a shout, a leap into the air, and then a dive to the floor! And how often we have seen that youngster penalized by being asked to sit on the sidelines until he thinks he can run without falling down! What this does is to rob him of the high spot of his enjoyment —the climax, making impossible the development of his play into an art form.

What we should do in a situation of this kind is to help the child learn how to take his climaxes and then to return to an even keel. We need to help him to a better and more artistic use of that form. If his running, for example, is accompanied by playing on drums, his climax can be accented by a corresponding climax on the drums, or perhaps by a crash of the gong. Among the many varieties of such play are different ways of falling, ways of getting up again, the use of the time when down as a part of the whole activity, crescendo and decrescendo of movement, and the use of the voice. The reader will find *The Rhythm Book* by Elizabeth Waterman [5] very helpful in its analysis of movement and of the direction in which it should develop.

The possibilities as well as the limitations of percussion instruments are discussed by Harriett Graham,[6] who points out that they should not be used exclusively because they do not furnish a fitting accompaniment to certain types of dance. It is true that continued use of them can become monotonous since they deal largely in the rhythmic element of music. We can, however, vary our use somewhat by adding different kinds of percussion instruments, or by the way we combine those we have. A keen ear will discover many variations in sound, depending on the way the instruments are played. Since there will be times when a piano is not available, or when the grown-up does not know how to play, a thoughtful use of percussion can add greatly to the musical and dance development of children. The outdoors is an ideal place for rhythmic play for little children, and these instruments offer an accompaniment that can *be taken to* children.

Skill in playing drums can, as we know, be developed to a high degree. Though this is not the place to discuss technique, certain fundamentals may be mentioned. In order to obtain an easy, relaxed rhythm, we must first feel the rhythm of the movement in our bodies. The rhythm on the drum should be the product of this feeling, and not the tapping out of the time beat.

A sensitive player can obtain good results in the quality of tone produced by remembering to "pull the sound out" of the

[5] Barnes.

[6] "A Study of the Use of Percussion Instruments as Accompaniment in the Dance." *Research Quarterly of the American Physical Education Association,* March 1934.

drum rather than beat it in. Moreover, as we pointed out in Chapter II, there are many ways of playing: slapping, or using the hollow hand, the fingers, or a wire brush. The sides yield various sounds, as do different parts of the drumhead. Regular tympani sticks are best, and here again there are various ways to use them, such as playing with the hard end or with the padded end.

For most of us, improvising on drums will be found much easier than improvising on a piano. Yet a working knowledge of the basic elements of musical structure need be no formidable hurdle to jump. Most of us are not among the lucky few who can sit down at a piano and improvise without any knowledge of the symbols of music; they are lucky in being more experimental and sound-minded than we. But if our piano teachers had had the imagination and courage to teach us first through the "raw materials" of music—sound and rhythm, we might from the beginning have established that feeling of at-homeness with the keyboard and that feeling of security which no amount of "playing pieces" could have given us. Some teachers are working in this direction with children, but too few use the same approach with older people. One does not need to be a creative genius to improvise, for improvisation is largely pure invention, and an immediate acquaintance with the theory of music gives us considerable on which to build.

In using the piano as accompaniment, we are able to bring to movement the added elements of harmony and melody that are not possible with drums. A few simple chords may be just what are needed to add substance to a group of four-year-old "tugboats." Occasions will arise, however, when improvising is far from adequate, and when even the person with a fairly extensive repertory cannot summon just the right music to fit the child's movement, though she knows that to round it out music must play a more important role. When this happens, she will (even though she may improvise temporarily rather than lose the spirit and enthusiasm of the child's idea) at the earliest possible moment search for music that will add more meaning to the child's experience.

It is not difficult to find music to accompany activity of a purely rhythmic character—that is, movement not tied up with content or idea. Our richest source for this is the field of folk music. The music of simple folk games, songs, and dances makes excellent accompaniment for such activities as running, jumping, skipping, galloping, marching, and swinging. It is simple, well accented, and (best of all) easy to play. It responds to the child and the child instinctively responds to it.

Many pieces that are similarly rhythmical have been written by a number of the great composers, some being excerpts from longer compositions. For the accompanist's use several collections of these have been made, the compilers having carefully edited and sometimes skillfully simplified the music so that it is not beyond the ability of the average pianist. Generally speaking, the simpler the musical accompaniment, the easier it is for the child to respond—and the more likely it is that the music will be well played. Music for accompaniment must be played clearly and evenly, and be well accented, with regard also for the longer line of its phrasing; and it is always of prime importance that the accompanist be keenly sensitive to the tempo and mood of the child or the group, and adjust her playing to that tempo and mood.

What about interpretation of music? Should one never play music first, asking the child to listen to it and then to do what "the music tells him"? We believe that this approach to music and dance has been greatly overworked and has resulted in sterile ideas and artificial form. If one is referring to the interpretation of the *mood* or *spirit* of the music, there are certainly times when the older child, especially, will enjoy this approach. But if one means the interpretation of the *content* of the music, one must make sure of letting the child be the judge of what the music means *to him.* The same music means different things to different people, and we are on dangerous ground when we try to interpret it for others. There have been cases in which two or more composers have treated the same idea, but their musical interpretations of that idea have been widely different.

An amusing incident illustrating a child's interpretation of music was told by a teacher from the Northwest. She had played music from Mendelssohn's *Midsummer Night's Dream* to accompany fairy dancing, and the groups had responded like fairies—all but one little boy, who had recently moved into the community from Florida. Every time the music was played he sat in a stiff huddle in the middle of the room, and no amount of talking about the way the music sounded had any effect on him. Finally the teacher asked: "But if the music does not make you want to be a fairy, what *are* you?" "I'm a frozen milk bottle—the music makes me think of *that!*" said the four-year-old from the Deep South. He had been intrigued, day after day, by the bottle of milk left on his kitchen doorstep—which was always frozen when it was taken in; and for some reason the "fairy" music had stimulated him to dramatize a frozen milk bottle!

A number of collections of dramatic music published for use with children can be very helpful to a teacher if she chooses from them judiciously. For instance, a composer or an editor has named a piece of music *Airplanes,* and it has been used successfully by some child or group to support their play—but this does not guarantee that the piece will fit other children's airplane play. If the teacher feels that a given child needs music of a dramatic character, she should first find out from him what kind he wants, and then play several selections for him that seem to her to fit his play, and let him be the judge of what he wants to use. Likewise, if a child chooses to interpret "elephant" music by rolling over and over to the rhythmic flow of the music, we should encourage his interpretation rather than insist on his "being an elephant" by walking on all fours or swinging his trunk.

When we give the children a chance to hear a variety of good music from which they can choose what seems to them most fitting for their play, we make them conscious of the music itself and more discriminating in their choice. It is then that we are really encouraging *good listening.*

This discussion has stressed the importance of working from movement rather than from music. Neither approach should be used to the exclusion of the other; but it has been our experience that, if we want a child to grow creatively in the field of dance, and at the same time want music to have real significance for him, we shall stress more and more the former approach rather than the latter. If the approach is from movement, the child will build up a truly rich background in both dance and music.

In conclusion it may be repeated that we are concerned with general experiences in the whole area of movement, rather than with steps or specific patterns. If we can help children to set dance processes in motion, to give congruous expression to their strong emotions through dance, if we can help them to find in dance a bridge between strenuous exercise and imagination, then movement will be a really satisfying and creative art medium in their lives.

Children approach music through their interest in sound, and, in the same way, they approach dance through their instinctive interest in movement

Courtesy Life Magazine

A musical visit from a double bass, an instrument that introduces children to entirely different types and ranges of sound

Getting personally acquainted with a harp

There is no one method, no one system, that will accomplish this. We must have broad vision, must use our imagination along with that of the child, and recognize the *educative value of progressive growth in an art rather than the final product.* Our most important contribution to this whole process is our attitude toward the art of dance. We are responsible for building the environment in which we work and live with children —an environment that will foster a genuine respect not only for the art of movement but for all the arts.

MUSIC COLLECTIONS

Here are listed some collections of music containing pieces for accompanying a great variety of children's movements. The song books, especially, will be found helpful to those who work with very young children.

Elizabeth Burchenal and C. W. Crampton. *Folk Dance Music.* Schirmer

Satis Coleman and Alice Thorn. *Singing Time.* John Day

—— *Another Singing Time.* John Day

Angela Diller and Kate S. Page. *A Pre-School Music Book.* Schirmer

—— *The Schubert Band Book.* Schirmer

Mabelle Glenn, Helen Leavitt, and Victor Rebmann. *Play a Tune.* Ginn

Mary Nancy Graham (compiler). *Fifty Favorite Songs for Boys and Girls.* Whitman

Edwin Hughes. *Master Series for the Young.* Schirmer (Bach, Beethoven, Schuman, Schubert, Mozart)

Ellen P. MacCartney. *Songs for the Nursery School.* Willis
Ethel Robinson. *School Rhythms.* Summy
Ruth Crawford Seeger. *American Folk Songs for Children.* Doubleday
Elizabeth Waterman. *ABC of Rhythmic Training.* Summy
Virginia B. Whitlock. *Come and Caper.* Schirmer

REFERENCE BOOKS ON DANCE

John Martin. *Introduction to the Dance.* Norton

6

CONCERTS

How MANY of us are on direct speaking terms with a bull fiddle, or have so much as touched the manual of a pipe organ, let alone pulled out stops, stepped on pedals, or played on two keyboards at the same time? How many of us are personally acquainted with a harp, or with a concert-size marimba?

Deep inside all of us grown-ups there is—if we but admit it —the same urge that a child has to feel and to handle, to touch and to try the new and unfamiliar, but we have learned to control it. It isn't only Junior who thrills when he "pulls out" an accordion; Daddy is just as eager to have his turn playing it as he is to run Junior's electric train! It isn't only Sister who strokes the ballet dancer's light, filmy skirt; Mother, too, comes in surreptitiously for her share of "the feel of the goods."

This desire to get on speaking terms with an artistic experience is instinctive in young and old. A visit backstage, a ringside seat at a night club, a coveted invitation to an afternoon of chamber music in a private home—all are occasions that adults look forward to and do not forget. And so we can easily understand how much it means to a child to be in "on the ground floor" at concerts as well as in other experiences.

In families who have musical friends or who are music-makers themselves, close contacts with players and instruments will occur as a matter of course in the children's lives. Two things are essential, however: first, there must be no sense of hurry in these contacts—they should be as leisurely as possible; and, second, the child should naturally have supervision, not in showing him how to play but in seeing that he uses the musical instrument so that no harm may come to it. When a youngster discovers some ingenious and unconventional way of making sounds with an instrument, it is hard for the adult not to say: "But *this* is the way to do it!" So that supervision must be largely a matter of self-control on the latter's part. On the whole, little children pretty much live up to what is expected of them, and they are quick to appreciate and respect the desirability of using an instrument carefully.

People who make music are not always easy to find, but it has been our experience that if one is sufficiently broadminded about what constitutes a musical experience interesting and unusual opportunities are sure to come.

What are some of the possible sources of music in an average community? Probably nothing delights a child more than to be able to sit on an organ bench and give himself over to soundmaking. He may not find Sullivan's "lost chord," but for him there is magic in the way this majestic instrument responds to his touch. A sympathetic and understanding organist who is willing to give some time to children occasionally, making it possible for them to get close to the organ and try it, will be rewarded not only by their enthusiastic interest but also by their keen ears when it is his turn to make music.

For the child, the success of these first contacts with an organ or with any other instrument will be in proportion to the player's willingness to let the child discover in his own way. The youngster does not want to be told—he wants to *find out for himself,* and enabling him to do this under the most favorable circumstances is a guarantee of the best kind of lesson. It goes without saying that no intelligent person would withhold pertinent information when the learner is ready to profit by it.

Another musical attraction the community offers is its church bells. Perhaps there is only a single bell, but what a thrill a tug on the rope can give a child! The writer well remembers as a high spot of her childhood the time when she was allowed to play "Amen" on the church chimes by pulling down the old-fashioned levers. Bells had a new meaning after that! There is nothing more fascinating to anyone than a visit to a bell or carillon tower, even if it isn't possible to play the bells.

All over the country our communities are becoming more and more music-conscious; many of them have organized bands, orchestras, or choral groups. Surely we should be able to tap some of these resources to bring children into closer contact with instruments and artists. Perhaps a member of an orchestra would be willing to come to a small group of children either at home or at school; or, if it is a question of some larger instruments like percussion, the children could go to the place where these are stored. If the group is small enough, each child can try out the instrument and then listen to it being played.

High school boys and girls are busy, we know, but we believe that those who play in the school orchestra would enjoy an occasional musical excursion either individually or in small groups to the rooms of the younger children in the school. If these music times are to be successful, it is important to work with a few children at a time, not with large groups, so as to give each child an opportunity to touch and to try.

Many music schools would probably be glad to co-operate

in introducing little children to musical instruments. This plan would have to be used wisely; obviously its purpose would not be to encourage the children to take lessons on any particular instrument, or to elicit admiring exclamations over the genius of some child prodigy. But in the long run any experience that gives music more meaning to children will eventually produce in them a heightened interest in learning music.

One of our most delightful music times in school occurred when a father brought his French horn and played for us. Here was an instrument that (for hygienic reasons) could not be "tried" in the usual sense of the word; but just to be able to hold it and admire its shine and its shape was satisfaction aplenty. We listened with both eyes and ears to its wonderful music; for many of the children it was the first hearing of Siegfried's horn call. Most of the time, however, was taken up by the playing of familiar songs on request.

There is nothing lovelier to hear than a well-played flute. With the exception, perhaps, of the violin, it does more to bring a lift in clearness and direction to a child's singing voice than any other instrument. In recent years, the "recorder" (fipple flute) has achieved considerable popularity among amateur musicians. It is fairly easy to learn to play, and its sweet, quiet tone provides a different type of musical experience for children.

Violin and 'cello are always enjoyed. Both these instruments lend themselves particularly well to the playing of familiar songs, and the child not only enjoys singing along with the instrument but also likes to listen. He is interested, too, in using his ears to help in the tuning and in discovering what happens when the mute is used. Unexpected questions come up, too. We especially like to recall the four-year-old who, after watching intently and listening to a visiting 'cellist play Christmas carols, asked her if a mouse had ever crawled into the hole in the 'cello!

Probably one of the experiences that will live longest in the memories of our five- and six-year-old children was the time when a double bass came to live with us for several weeks. Here *was* a musical visit—the kind of visit that really meant something. Day after day the children had ample opportunity to get acquainted with this old fellow, and from time to time Mother and Father, Grandmother and Grandfather, Little Sister and Brother were brought to school to see and to play on the great fiddle. The student to whom the instrument belonged had a hard time keeping up with the children's requests, for here was an instrument with an entirely different type and range of sound. Together with a violin played by a teacher, a piano, and the children's voices, we had some exciting times in putting sounds together. *Hickory Dickory Dock* lent itself well to our orchestration, some of the children "clucking" the tick-tock along with the plucked bass strings, and the violin and piano carrying the melody with a group of children singing. We had great fun, too, with *Old Macdonald Had a Farm,* the children deciding which instruments—voice, violin, bass, or piano—would best interpret the various animal sounds.

One day a Marine and his accordion came to school. He had the faculty of making himself at home immediately and, pulling a stool up by the fire, he was halfway through *The Marines' Hymn* before most of the children realized he was there. The audience was so swept off its feet by his music-making that he had played several songs before requests came for favorites. Here was an experience full of the strength of a fighting youth—an experience that in turn evoked from the children a quality of listening too rarely aroused in an adult concert audience. The playing of *Old Zip Coon* incited some of them to dance, but the majority were more interested in listening and especially in watching this Marine and his instrument, only occasionally joining in a song.

Possibilities for strikingly unusual musical experiences may be uncovered quite unexpectedly. A few years ago a trip on a Staten Island ferry boat was made delightfully enlivened by the entertainment provided by an old Negro who played on a group of different-sized bowls of uncertain pitch, arranged according to his own "special scale" on a wobbly card table. This itinerant musician, carrying his table and his bag of bowls with him, gave his concerts on street corners in various sections of the city. He was only too glad to come and play for our children, his calm dignity and self-respect convincingly corroborating his simple statement that he was "born a genius."

A Scotch bagpiper, in return for a contribution to his war ambulance fund, left his traveling automobile concert stage to come into our room one rainy day when it was too wet for us to stand outside and hear him play. Since bagpipes make a big sound, he suggested, after letting the children examine his instrument, that they stay at one end of the large room while he played to them from the other end. But after one number, he found it hard to stand still and he marched around the room playing martial airs followed by the children. This was truly an inspiring experience for all of us.

A special treat for the last day of school one spring was provided by the visit of an organ grinder and his hand organ. As it was a cool day he had left his monkey at home—at least, this was the explanation he gave to the children. But he had been engaged the day before, and he may have had other reasons for not exposing his monkey to kindergarten. In any case, the monkey's absence was undoubtedly a distinct advantage from the point of view of a musical experience! The organ grinder was a friendly and patient person. Opening the top of his music box, he let every child not only grind out music but also watch what happened on the inside as the metal records turned round.

Such are only a few of a great variety of musical experiences that it has been possible to bring to our children. Naturally some years produce a richer harvest than others, but we have had few really lean ones. To our parents goes a great deal of the credit for bringing in not only their own talents but those of their friends. Not long ago a father who is a dentist persuaded a guitar-playing patient to play and sing for us. A mother brought in a friend who knows a vast number of our country's folk songs, and we not only heard some unfamiliar ones but discovered that we were already acquainted with many of her favorites.

Another parent beguiled a Russian dancer whom she had met at a dinner party to come and entertain us. He rose to the occasion by appearing in costume. His dancing plus his infectious personality will not soon be forgotten. But our "amateur" experiences are not forgotten, either. Some years ago a friend who indulged in tap dancing purely for his own enjoyment visited us and danced for the children. Before he left, he showed the children a little dance called "Sugar on the Toe" in which one foot brushed lightly over the toe of the other foot. Five years later two of our boys, passing this man on the street, stopped to greet him, "*You* remember," one of them reminded the other; "this is the man who danced 'Sugar on the Toe'!"

All over the country there is increasing awareness of the need for bringing school and community into closer relationship with each other. Too long has the emphasis been solely on acquainting the parents with the school. Though this is important, it is high time that the school should acquaint itself with the parents and realize some of the valuable assets that are lying dormant in every community. Co-operation is a two-way process, and the more we can call upon parents to lend their talents and abilities to the school, the richer are the experiences we can offer to the children, to say nothing of the value of the relationship among parent, child, and teacher that inevitably emerges. There will be no gap to bridge between school and community if these person-to-person contacts are established, taken advantage of, and respected.

The parents and friends who lend their talents for our little concerts have a thoroughly enjoyable time, but we also notice that, if the children have any advance notice of a musical visit, a surprising number of mothers drop in at "music time." These informal experiences have been so much enjoyed by all that we have had many requests to recommend "regular" concerts to which parents can take their children. Mothers reported that the "Children's Concerts" in New York City were primarily designed for older children and were not suited to the younger ones' stage of development; and that the audiences were too large, the programs over long, and the seats uncomfortable for short legs. Yet these mothers believed that their children were ready for something of the kind, and did not know where to find that something.

Neither did we, and so, together with a group of interested parents, we decided to give our own series of concerts for little children on a professional basis, employing suitable talent and charging admission. There was no idea of substituting these concerts for our informal experiences, but rather we saw in them a way to supplement and enlarge the musical horizon of our children.

In planning these concerts, we began thinking back to our day-by-day experiences with children and music, trying to determine the reasons why children bring so much interest and enthusiasm to their listening. We knew we must retain these if the new venture was to be successful.

First of all we recognized the importance of "nearness," which demanded reasonably small groups in a setting that offered an intimate chamber-music atmosphere. Fortunately we have the use of a large room. The children's chairs were arranged in a wide semicircle, and the artists appeared, not on a distant stage, but on the same floor level and directly in front of the audience. Comfortable seats obviated the restlessness that results when short legs dangle; and ease in seeing and hearing did away with stirring and moving about. The parents sat on larger chairs directly behind the children.

A second important point was recognition of the fact that children cannot sit still for very long at a time; they simply aren't made that way. This meant planning a short program that would be well within their span of attention, rather than trying to hold their interest beyond its natural limits. Our experience had proved that a half-hour program, containing a short "intermission" period, is about long enough for groups of young children. Not that there weren't always requests for more music; sometimes the children sat so tight to their chairs after the final number that if we had not been careful we might easily have been persuaded to let the programs grow longer. Naturally our plans were flexible, and an occasional encore took care of any unusual interest. But we kept watching for the subtle signs of a group's reaction, and held it safer to err on the short rather than on the long side. The audience ought to go home wanting more—that is good psychology whether applied to young or to old.

For the children, an intermission has value not only because it gives them an opportunity to get up and walk about and talk with their friends, but especially because they get a chance to meet the artists and see the instruments at close hand. They need a little help from time to time in learning how to use this free time to the best advantage of all, but the achievement of a good balance between freedom and self-control constitutes one of the most important aspects of the whole experience. Success here depends largely on the children's knowing that each one will have an opportunity to get close to what is going on, if not during the intermission then after the concert is over. Occasionally it is possible to have the instrument on hand before the concert, as in the case of a harp that was rented by the school for several weeks and kept in the music studio; thus every child had unhurried time in which to try out the fascinating instrument. For one of our programs the artist assembled her marimba during the morning while the kindergarten children were in the room. She had a most attentive audience as well as many suggestions as to how it should be put together! After it was set up, each child had plenty of time to play on it, nor did the adults in the room miss out on their turns!

Perhaps the most thought-provoking part of a concert venture for young children is the planning of the program content. Here we proceeded on the assumption that children like music for its own sake, that its appeal comes to them directly through the medium of sound and rhythm, and that it is essentially a sensory and not an intellectual experience. We considered the "commentator" out of place at a children's concert, just as he is at a concert for grown-ups. Why should we tell children what the music is going to sound like? Are we afraid that they are not going to react in our way or in the way the critics tell us to react? Let's give youngsters a chance to feel for themselves—or not feel, if that happens to be their disposition. And so there was no *talking about music* at our concerts, for we believed with the late Oscar Thompson that "the highest degree of musical appreciation comes through the plain direct speech of music itself." [1] We showed no pictures; we told no stories; we did not ask children to listen for this or that; we did not talk about the composer. In other words, there was no build up for the concert itself, though there *was* a build-up—a day-by-day one, a lasting one—that came from the children's continuous interest in sound and rhythm and from our seizing every opportunity to foster it.

It was not easy to know in advance what music would have the greatest appeal. Certain guiding principles, however, helped us to choose. Gay, spirited music was always enjoyed, and here we could draw from the modern as well as the classical composers, for "modern" harmonies are much more likely to be accepted by youngsters than by older people. A very short group of pieces by Hindemith at a string-quartet concert and Salzedo's *Chanson dans la nuit* for the harp both received enthusiastic response.

Children are affected by the mass of tone produced as well as by the melody and rhythm of music. Mursell calls attention to this in his chapter on "The Psychology of Music Listening": "Not only children but many adults are affected by the sheer mass of the tone and this takes precedence over both rhythmic structure and melodic design. In this kind of listening we have the ultimate foundation of all music." [2]

Balance in each program was achieved through planning a succession of contrasting numbers, as well as through including

[1] Oscar Thompson. *How to Understand Music*. Dial.
[2] James L. Mursell. *The Psychology of Music*. Norton.

several that were already familiar to the children. When it was a singing concert, the children frequently joined in their favorite songs—though this was always spontaneous, not directed. A child may prefer to just listen to a favorite song sung by an artist, or he may be inspired to sing, too. At the instrumental and dance concerts the children were always given the opportunity to participate by singing one or two songs.

We have been extremely fortunate in working closely with understanding artists who have helped in arranging the programs. These musicians have been unusually sensitive to the children's responses; and they have had genuine respect for the children's musical intelligence. Our concerts have been informal, yet at the same time dignified, with no playing down to the audience and no attempt to hold its attention by coy remarks. Our sincere desire has been to encourage "good listening." If music has to compete with inattention and lack of interest, then something is wrong with our programs.

Just as we try to offer a balanced diet within each program, so we plan for a variety of musical experiences in any given season. A series of three programs is given each year on alternate Friday afternoons in January and February, each one being repeated for the older children of the school on the same afternoon and in the same place, but at a different hour. The five-, six-, and seven-year-olds make up the younger group. The division into a younger and an older group is made in order to keep the size of the audience relatively small. Children under the age of five are not admitted because we believe in general that they are not ready for a group experience of this kind.

Three types of concerts have been given each year: singing, instrumental, and dance. The singing concerts have offered a wide range of music: American and South American folk songs accompanied by guitar, foreign folk songs and ballads, Gilbert and Sullivan, short operatic arias, and Negro spirituals. Over a period of several years a large variety of instruments have been presented: harp, flute, marimba, harmonica, violin, viola, 'cello, and piano—and one concert was devoted exclusively to percussion. Our dance concerts have included a Russian group accompanied by balalaika and accordion, a program of contemporary dance, and a ballet program in which the beautiful dancer had to be rescued from her ardent admirers during intermission time and placed on a table so as to be seen by all—one little boy offering to hold her up if she would stand on her toes!

What do we expect children to gain from these concerts? First of all, we want to make sure that they do not come to music too late, that they do not miss out on at-homeness with the best in music during their early plastic years. Children are capable of seeing and hearing actively. They are not consciously storing away immediate experiences merely for the purpose of adding to their repertories and becoming "cultured." Immediate results are not directly aimed at nor even thought about, but there has been a sincere desire to live up to children's musical potentialities. Children must be left free to feel about music, each in his own particular way. We do not ask questions about it, nor on the other hand do we hesitate to talk with them about it or help to extend their information and understanding if they seem to want this. We try always to remember, however, that *verbal responses are not necessarily indicative of music appreciation.*

The success of our concerts has been in large measure due to the enthusiastic support of the parents. From the very beginning we have been able to count on their understanding and their very practical help, not only in searching for artists and in giving of their own talents, but also in such very important matters as the set-up and arrangement of the room and the numerous details that accompany taking care, comfortably, of large groups of children and adults.

After our first two seasons of concerts, our Parent Teachers Association became so interested in our project that it voted to give us financial support. Its generosity has enabled us to secure musical talent at regular professional rates and has given us access to a wider field of experiences than would otherwise have been possible. We may be prejudiced, but we cannot think of a more valuable contribution for a Parent Teachers Association to make than assistance in a school project of this nature.

We do not, however, want to give the impression that concert experiences for little children depend upon the amount of money expended. Each community has its own resources (many of them unique), and the discovering and utilization of these could very well be the most exciting and rewarding aspect of bringing more music to children.

We cannot close this chapter without referring to the comments and reactions of the artists who have brought their talents to us. They have, every one of them, declared that never did they have such enthusiastic and attentive audiences. They are likely at first to attribute the absence of behavior problems to training and discipline, but we point out quickly that this is not the case. Children respond with the best that is in them to that which is right for them. What is for them a full and satisfying experience is the result of our recognizing the limitations due to their stage of growth.

The organ is a magical instrument to a child

Feeling the vibrations of a kettledrum

Courtesy Parents' Magazine

The trombone makes unexpected sounds

The importance of "closeness" in concerts for children

PICTURE BOOKS OF INSTRUMENTS

Harriet E. Huntington. *Tune Up.* Doubleday, Doran. Lovely photographs of the instruments of the orchestra and their players.

Marion Lacey, illus. Leonard Weisgard. *Picture Book of Musical Instruments.* Lothrop, Lee & Shepard.

7
MUSIC AND THE CLASSROOM TEACHER

THE MOST important factor in children's musical development is the attitude towards music of the people with whom they live. In the school this person is the classroom teacher, for it is with this teacher that the child spends the major part of his school day. Does this teacher hear music in children's sound making; does she feel dance in children's natural use of movement as they go about their daily work; does she have a quick ear for a child's humming of a song as he browses, works, or plays, especially if it is a song not in the music course of study; is her understanding of what constitutes music constantly growing and expanding? Is she wide awake to her own musical possibilities, or does she shut off any use of her own resources by feeling inadequate because she cannot play an instrument or perhaps occasionally sings off key? Is she the kind of person who is willing to jump in and do the best she can with what she has; is she at ease with children *and her coworkers* so that she can make mistakes—even enjoy them—and learn from them? Or is she the master or perfectionist teacher who is ever on guard against making a mistake and thus stunts her own growth to say nothing of the unfortunate mental hygiene aspects of an environment for children which result from being taught by this "all complete" person? These characteristics naturally apply to all aspects of school life, but it is necessary to remember that in providing a good musical life for children we must be concerned with the child's total day and not just music periods.

CLASSROOM TEACHERS HAVE SKILLS. Teachers need to be alert to and have respect for their own ways of making music and utilize their resources with children. The following incident illustrates my point. A short while ago I participated in a music workshop on the campus of a large southwestern university. One morning in search of a respite from work I found a quiet corner of the campus, and while enjoying the wide green spaces and listening to the birds, I was suddenly aware of a "bird" right back of me. Turning around there was one of the teachers who was studying at the workshop who also felt the need for relaxation. But she was enjoying herself by whistling birds calls. "Fun, isn't it?" she asked. "But where did you ever learn to do such whistling? You can match those calls perfectly," I replied in astonishment. "Oh, I have always whistled, I guess. My mother used to whistle when she churned butter, usually to the tune of *When the Roll Is Called up Yonder;* and my sister and I learned from her. Only we always were much more elaborate in our whistling. We really improved on Mother!" "Your third graders must think you are a pretty wonderful teacher, and I can well imagine the good whistling times you have together," I responded. "But—but," she replied, "I have never whistled in school and I have been teaching for twenty years and part of that time I taught music, but I just never thought of whistling being 'school music.' It was never mentioned in the course of study. Do you really think it is all right?" she asked breathlessly, and without waiting for my reply, she went on, "I can't wait for school to begin next fall."

Here was a truly musical person who had never called upon her own unique talent because of her concept of school music. It is inconceivable that any music supervisor would have objected to her using this talent, but, on the other hand, no one had ever taken the trouble to encourage her to exploit her own resources. Certainly, no course of study intends to set limits on the teacher, but no one has yet seemed to have found the answer to the problem of discovering what the teacher already has or what she is especially fitted for musically. And this will never happen as long as we think of music in terms of a few categories! If we continue to use the usually accepted musical measuring stick to discover the teacher's musicianship, we shall never take advantage of many of these talents which teachers have. Does this mean that this teacher will, for example, have only whistling music in her room? Certainly not, for to the extent that she is a person who finds satisfaction and joy in releasing her own talents, she will, in turn, be better able to appreciate the necessity for having equal respect for the musical talents of each child in her room. Together teacher and children will be eager to reach out for new experiences.

CHILDREN HAVE SKILLS, TOO. How can we live with children so that they know that we are honestly interested in their musical interests? Recently I observed a session where a group of eleven- and twelve-year-olds were having a guessing contest on radio commercials. Each child would tap out on his desk the rhythm of a particular commercial, and the others would guess which one it was. In this contest the teacher came out at the bottom of the class! The children were quick, too, in identifying similarities in rhythm with well-known pieces of music. This same teacher happens to be particularly fond of Bach's *St. Matthew Passion,* and one day while writing some work on the chalk board was humming some of the more familiar passages to herself. One of the children said, "What is that, Miss F.?" "Oh, it's some music that I like," and she named it. "Sing it again," asked several children. She did, and then they asked her if she would bring the phonograph record of this music to school. She did but doubted if it would really appeal to them. However, she was amazed at the interest they brought to it, and they have asked for certain parts of it over and over. This teacher does not play an instrument or even sing well, but her children have a rich musical environment because it is a place where each person lives at ease and feels that what he has to offer is of worth.

BOTH TIME AND UNDERSTANDING ARE NEEDED. This means, of course, that time must be allotted in the school day for such experiences. Certainly some days will yield more than others, but children soon catch the spirit of a classroom to which they can bring what is important to them. Along with time, and perhaps even more important, is an atmosphere of permissiveness where children's immediate interests and emotional feelings are respected by the teacher, such as the following incident in a third-grade room illustrates.

The children had just returned from a good time on the playground and were lively, talkative and exuberant. Suddenly one youngster started singing *Yippy Ti Yi Yo.* All joined in at once, and it was clearly evident that no football cheer leaders ever sang with more fervor. The teacher, however, waved her hand, and everyone stopped while she went to her desk and extracted a pitch pipe from the drawer. "We must be sure to sing in the right key," and then proceeded to give them the pitch of the song. By this time cold water had been thrown on the group's enthusiasm and feeling for singing, and the result was straggling and limpid. Now the fact that the group felt free enough to start singing on their own is a fine commentary on the friendly atmosphere that existed in this room. For this, the teacher is to be commended. Also she was eager to follow the children's lead and only sought to do a good job of guidance. But in this case she found herself dealing only with the perfection of the product at an inopportune time, neglecting the buoyant spirits that had motivated the singing. Should there be no guidance then? Most certainly there should be, but in this instance rather than promoting the quality of the music experience the "guidance" terminated that experience. In dealing with children's enthusiasms (and we are not talking about a case where a child is out to make trouble) we must have appreciation for children's ways of doing things. The chances are good that out of a repetition of this song would have come more control on the part of the children, especially if the teacher had joined in and had forgotten about the "right" way to sing the song.

Let us examine this illustration further. Somewhere as a part of her training this teacher had been told that songs must always be sung in the same key, and since she was not sure of herself, she felt it necessary to depend on a pitch pipe. The important thing about singing a song is to sing it in a key that is comfortable—a key that is within the range of the average group voices. It would be more than a little ridiculous, if people always carried a pitch pipe with them when they sing on picnics, at games, around camp fires, etc. Occasionally a song gets started a bit too high or too low, but nobody minds, and they start over again. By trial and error they find the best singing place. Children are able to do this, too. In fact, this can be an excellent opportunity for them to learn in the same way. If it does not work the first time, try again. At certain times children might also be interested in learning about the matter of different keys through the use of a piano, xylophone, and pitch pipe. The point that needs to be made here is that it is not a choice between no guidance or guidance, between no learning or learning, but rather a sensing of what comes first and meeting the situation in such a way as not to dampen children's interest and thereby cut off any possibility for growth. In this particular case the teacher's goal for perfection spoiled a musical experience.

USE AND DEVELOPMENT OF MUSIC RESOURCES. It is important that teachers, children, and schools be constant discoverers and even exploiters in this matter of music resources. What may seem to be an almost barren environment musically speaking, as looked at through the limited concept of music existing in too many schools, may well turn out to be rich in possibilities. Here we have to think of such things as variety of music experiences, use of equipment already owned by the school, freedom from grade-level approach, possibilities of renting or borrowing suitable instruments, and enlisting the co-operation of parents and laymen in the community as discussed in Chapter 6.

VARIETY OF EXPERIENCES. The examples discussed in the early part of Chapter 6 illustrate varieties of music possibilities, but I should like to add one more. A teacher in a small midwestern town tells of a most rewarding year musically. Her father frequently told his family how much he enjoyed his visits to the town barber because he combined his trade with the singing of operatic arias! The fact that his voice was not equal to all of the operatic demands concerned neither him nor his customers. Here was the "natural" that teacher had been looking for, and when she asked him if he would come and sing with her first and second grades, he was delighted. Most of the children knew him, but this special arrangement gave status not only to him as a person but also to music. He sang, of course, in Italian, and it was not long until he had help from the children in the easily singable parts of his arias. The enthusiasm for singing generated by this and later visits carried over into all of the children's musical activities. Perhaps, however, the most important overtones in this experience were in the field of human relationships!

FREEDOM FROM GRADE-LEVEL APPROACH. Most schools have one or more series of music books organized on grade levels. Some of these series contain an accumulation of excellent music. In general, they are planned and assembled on the principle of simple first and proceed to the more complicated. To some extent this principle has validity, but the important missing link in following such a system is that it neglects to take account of the one most important factor in learning, i.e., the motivation of the learner. Children learn what they want to learn, and many times one would expect these learnings to be way beyond their abilities. But youngsters have a way of coming through. Many a child who does not sing in school takes the latest song off the radio or phonograph record in his stride. (Certainly the ease with which children learn from radio and record should make us question and give serious thought to many of our present methods of teaching singing in schools.)

There is logic and continuity in the way children learn but the logic and continuity are in terms of what goes on *inside* the individual and may have nothing to do with simple to difficult or content relationship apparent to the teacher. It really hinges on what makes sense to the child. Psychologists have been telling us this for some time [1] but nowhere has it been more clearly and convincingly pointed out for the classroom teacher than by Alice Miel.[2] "Continuity in learning has been confused with sequence of activities or experiences as arranged mechanically for the learner by someone else. The fact has been overlooked that continuity in learning is an individual, internal affair; that the individual himself must see new relationships, new likenesses, and differences. In fact, arrangements made by the school often have made it more difficult for individuals to take the next steps in learning for which they are most ready. . . . Some individuals have been put under so much pressure to follow an externally imposed, artificial continuity that their own best sequence has been interrupted."

This understanding of the learning process has implications for the ways in which we use our music books. We might wish they were organized differently, but at least we can ignore the age-level classifications and use the books as source material searching and exploring together with children for music that has meaning for them regardless of their age. Many teachers are accustomed to following a music grade-level book and hesitate to change for fear of losing their bearings—it's important, too, for teachers to be secure. A teacher can, however, cultivate an awareness and tolerance of variations that children constantly offer even within a formal school situation and be willing to take a chance now and then, and thus gradually move out from where she is and eventually gain independence

[1] Snygg and Combs. *Individual Behavior.*
Mursell. *Education for Musical Growth.*

[2] Alice Miel. *Continuous Learning.* Bulletin No. 87. Association for Childhood Education International. P. 5.

from a system. The more willing she is to accept children's variations from the accustomed order of doing things, the more relaxed she becomes.

USE OF SCHOOL MUSICAL EQUIPMENT. Teachers within schools are learning more and more the benefits of working co-operatively with each other in the use of school equipment. Rather than allotting musical instruments to certain grades with the idea that these are the instruments to be used by this grade only because of the children's age, etc., both teachers and children should be able to turn to the total resources of the school. This cannot be done by rotating them mechanically. A principal of a ten-room school in Wyoming relates a unique and profitable use of the school's one piano. The spinet piano's home base is in the auditorium, but it spends most of its time visiting. Attached to ball-bearing rollers, it is easily moved from classroom to classroom according to children's needs. The length of its stay in any one room depends upon its use and the needs of other groups. The important thing in this situation is that the teachers are willing to allow time in the school day for the children to "play" the piano, especially those who have no piano at home or who have taken no piano lessons.

Another school for the past several years has been able to have an allowance in its budget for renting instruments. A harp was rented for a month and arrangements made so that each classroom had the loan of it for several days. This gave both children and teacher an opportunity to get acquainted with it first hand and play it in the ways they could play. At the end of this period a harpist gave a concert, playing some music chosen by the children. At another time a concert-size xylophone was rented and used in the same way followed by a concert. A great many elementary schools are unable to employ a special music teacher and yet may be able to have a moderate sum set aside for music. They could well supplement their program in ways as described. Children and teachers could plan together for a variety of informal music experiences and employ artists for a reasonable fee.

THE MUSIC CONSULTANT. In today's educational language the music supervisor has become the music consultant. This is the result of the trend in many schools toward a different concept of the role of the specialist. Unfortunately, some serious misunderstandings have come about both on the part of the classroom teacher and the specialist. The latter may feel her job is threatened and the former frequently feels inadequate in meeting children's needs in special areas such as music. Both are needed. What is at stake is a more economical way of working, a way more in keeping with the way in which children learn so that the competencies and skills of the specialist are used effectively.

What we call the music teacher may not be too important although the term consultant has significant connotations in defining her function. It is her way of working with people and her respect for the many varied and different degrees of ability in teachers that makes for a good music program in her school. Can she "spark" the classroom teacher musically? Is she willing to put aside her carefully prepared plans for a particular situation in the light of deeper and more immediate interests of children? Is she a learner in the matter of taking cues from the classroom teacher about a special group of children? A few years ago when the customary procedure in teaching music in a certain school included two visits a week to each classroom by the music teacher, there was a second grade in charge of an unusually creative sixty-year-old teacher. Now this teacher liked music in a reserved sort of way, but her enjoyment had been from the outside rather than feeling a part of it. A new music teacher arrived, and in a few months this classroom came alive musically as never before and Miss B., the teacher, found herself humming songs while she worked and even trying to pick out melodies on the piano—things she had never dared try before. How did it happen?

The music teacher was so impressed with Miss B.'s understanding of children that she made a point of dropping in to this room whenever she could to learn more about children and about teaching. She was accepted as a member of the group and frequently was called on to help with everything from teaching reading to helping at the workbench. This person was no longer a "music teacher" but first of all, a *teacher,* with a special skill, however, in music. It was an exciting year musically, too, and the children's musical growth was nothing short of spectacular.

This illustration shows the importance of the music teacher's taking time to learn about children—this time in a classroom situation and with their regular teacher. In the following account we have the interesting story of a musically educated person who volunteered to work in a neighborhood after-school program and thus learned about youngsters in a very different way. To begin with, unless she offered something of interest, she had no children to work with, for they did not have to come to this group. These children lived in a crowded section of New York City. After a few weeks she found herself both musically and physically exhausted and with a dwindling group of children. So she tried a different plan. She collected a number of large drums, making most of them herself out of barrels, kegs, wooden pails, etc., some wooden temple bells, gongs, and tambourines, and decided to let this group find out for themselves about these instruments. Here is her story.[3]

"A group of ten eleven-year-old boys and one girl came regularly twice a week for several months. Each day they started off drumming, each one as an individual at first, but soon they would become aware of each other and some group activity would develop. At first it was mostly Indian dancing. They used a large old scrap basket as the fire to dance around and also wandered all over the room. They thought up a play—some Indians drumming, some dancing, getting wilder and wilder, beating faster and faster, until at a sign from one of them they all collapsed around the 'fire' and slept. At this point they sometimes asked for sleeping music from the piano. They lay with their eyes shut, completely relaxed, for several minutes, then up and at it again.

"Having exhausted this idea, they went on to the army. They divided themselves into three groups, the United States, the enemy, and a drumming group for sound effects. They came from home loaded with 'props'—helmets, guns, pistols, knapsacks, canteens, and ammunition belts. After a great deal of discussion and planning of the play they ended up under the tables except for the drum crew and made sorties from time to time, crawling, then dashing only to be hit by one of the constant volleys of machine gun fire and exploding bombs. Their body movements when 'hit' were magnificent—a sudden stiffening, then a struggle, and an abandoned fall—quite reminiscent of many of Martha Graham's movements. Then the snooping enemy, the United States troops discovering them—all done in a mixture of stylized dance and realism, primitive and full of vitality but often surprisingly relaxed with an almost 'floopy' quality to their movements. They often ended these afternoons with demands to sing *Caissons,* the Army Air

[3] Used with permission of Louisa Harris.

Corps song, *Anchors Aweigh* and *John Brown's Baby Had a Cold upon Its Chest.*

"After several weeks of this play, they came in one afternoon and started jumping high in the air. They all seemed to have acquired springs in their shoes. During their usual preliminary session they decided to do tricks such as jumping over as many as five chairs laid down on the floor next to each other. They lined up and as they ran to the point of the take-off the drummers played a roll; then there was silence as they went through the air followed by a good resounding bang as they landed. Then they asked for circus music from the piano. They stood on their heads, or on their hands; some lay on their backs and kicked their legs; some marched around. All the time there was a drum beat as well as the piano. When the drummer felt like joining the active group, he would lay down his sticks, which would be picked up by someone else who needed a rest.

"Two weeks later, they suddenly thought of sending messages on their drums. They made up their own Morse code. One beat meant A, two beats B, and so on until they reached ten (J). This stumped them a bit, so I suggested that they beat once and then make a gesture with their hand for the zero. For H they decided on one loud beat followed by one soft. They followed through the alphabet this way and were soon busy with paper and pencil making copies of the code for everyone. Then they spent a fascinating afternoon beating out messages to each other. Suddenly Jimmy said, 'Wait a minute, listen!' Code was forgotten for the moment. 'Do you see how the sound goes on after it's hit?' They all listened while he showed them what he meant, and then they all experimented. David said, 'Yes, and my drum reverberates when you hit yours.' So they discovered sound waves, and we discussed them and likened them to ripples in a pool when you throw in stones. The rest of the period was spent in experimenting with sound, one drumming gently in the middle of the group while the rest listened intently, both hearing and feeling with their hands if their drums would reverberate. They moved away from the drummer until they discovered the place farthest away where they could still pick up the vibration."

IMPLICATIONS FOR MUSIC TEACHING. Are there some implications in this music teacher's interesting experience for those of us who work in schools? When she worked hard and conscientiously to "put across music," she found herself not only worn out but also without children. In order to hold these youngsters, she simply had to get on their side and first find out and then accept what was musically big with them. It took courage and it took faith to let them find their way. The first few sessions were LOUD and to the observer at first seemed overstimulating (until she became an active participant). It soon became apparent, however, that the contrary was true. These children were having an opportunity to work out their tensions through the use of primitive instruments that required no lessons on "how to play." In addition to the musical values in working in sound and rhythm, have we given enough consideration to the opportunities children need for "sound therapy"? Schools put a great premium on being quiet. Even the use of instruments is highly controlled, and yet what red-blooded youngster does not yearn for just one resounding whack at these sound-provoking instruments.

In spite of the explosiveness of the first few sessions with these groups there was order, in that each child was working out his own feelings on his own instrument and in his own way and never interfering with another. It was not long, however, until they began to relate to each other, and their own organization, as described above, evolved, which included the use of the special skills of the teacher. We all want children to like music, to find release, satisfaction, and enjoyment in it. If we are honest in wanting them to meet these needs, we must accept their ways of doing it. We must first of all get on their track. Perhaps some of our goals may even be the same, but the routes in reaching these goals are very different.

The music teacher, then, may work in a number of ways—serving small groups of interested children, working with classroom teachers so as to make them more comfortable musically, as a resource person to whom both children and teacher turn for help in materials, in instruments, and in skills. Plans for working in any particular school may include scheduled periods in the classroom by the music teacher or scheduled periods in the music room for the children, or no regularly scheduled visits—music needs being met entirely through individual planning or working entirely with teachers. The music teacher may be called consultant or supervisor. To the extent that both music and classroom teachers keep their ears to the ground in the matter of discovering and accepting children's *real* music interests, to the extent that they get on the same track with them, to the extent that they, too, are accepted members of the group *who also bring ideas and suggestions,* they will find countless opportunities to extend and broaden children's musical horizons. Music education then becomes a working together rather than a pouring-in process by the teacher. And so we come back to the point of this chapter and that is—THE KEY PERSON IN A GOOD MUSIC PROGRAM IS THE CLASSROOM TEACHER, FOR IT IS HER ATTITUDE TOWARDS MUSIC AND NOT HER TECHNICAL SKILL THAT IS RESPONSIBLE FOR THE MUSIC THAT GOES ON IN HER ROOM AND THAT WILL REMAIN WITH HER CHILDREN.

Planning by children and teacher allows time for music in their own classroom

Independence at three

Teachers are learners too

Pre-service students learning to play the guitar

Putting musical sounds together

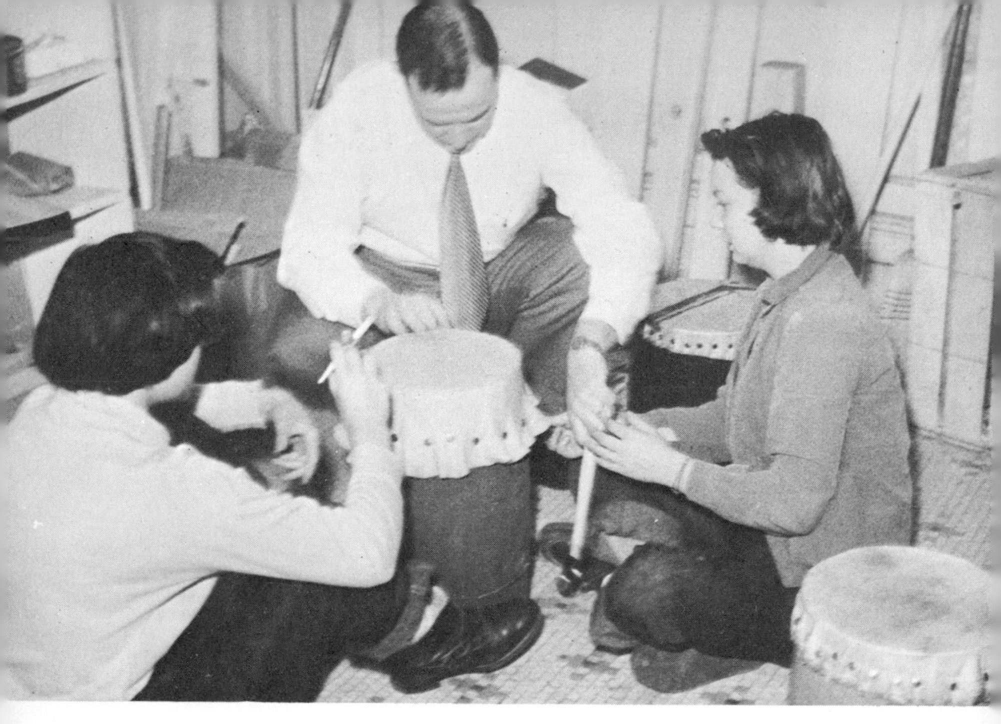

Teachers can make instruments

Teachers experimenting with movement and sound

8

MUSIC EXPERIENCES FOR TEACHERS

IF WE are going to be able to identify with and accept children's sound-making as a basis for their musical development, we must discover or perhaps rediscover our own skills in this field. And this takes courage. Our ability to grow in "comfortableness" in sound-making depends upon our degree of conformity to the traditional music pattern and to what society approves. Let us consider how we can go about this job. The following suggestions for ways of finding out more about music so that we can get closer to children are *most certainly not* to be interpreted as a system or method. They simply represent a very few of the possibilities the writer has discovered together with teachers and graduate students over a period of years, the majority of these people having been experienced classroom teachers with little or no technical skill in music.

GROUP SOUNDS. How do we increase our own perceptions in listening to sounds? Do you ever listen to the sounds of children's voices in a group? Are you able to relax enough to listen to sounds during a busy activity period in a classroom—variations in pitch, different rhythms, the timbre of voices en masse, gradations and changes almost rhythmical at times from much sound to a lull? When you call a group of children together for a meeting or a story at the end of a busy work period, they come bubbling over with matters important to them which they must share immediately with their friends. Confronted with this buzzing, can you relax and listen to these buzz groups feeling pretty certain that there will soon be enough of a lull for you to start the business of the hour? At the most, this waiting is usually only a matter of a few minutes, but it makes all the difference in the world in the kind of climate that exists in a group coming in a "natural way" to attention than is produced by a sharp "Attention please." It is interesting, too, how some of the children become aware of this waiting and react in opposite extremes from not only sensing pauses and trying to "shush" their neighbors to playing a game of outtalking teacher, which a teacher with a good sense of humor can appreciate and also handle. (We are not talking here about emergency situations that demand immediate attention from children, for no teacher has a right to live long with a group without planning and developing with them a way of securing immediate response when necessary.) These few minutes of waiting time pay dividends not only in terms of relaxation for teacher but also help in cultivating her ear for sound. And sometimes the thoughtful and *listening* teacher may decide that *these buzz groups*—and not what she had planned—are the important business of the hour!

BE-BOP AND BARTOK. Let us listen to the sharp staccato use of voices as children play. This, writes a music teacher [1] is more akin to be-bop than to our usually accepted music. "Children's

[1] Used by permission of Arnold Caswell.

own original songs, hums, chants, and piano pieces tend to be cast in rhythmic patterns and tonal patterns which are most sensible and interesting to the accomplished be-bop musician and to the successful composer who feels at home in the modern idiom. In order to foster musical growth, I believe it is important that the classroom teacher recognize and use contemporary music in the classroom, and I also suggest that contemporary music is much closer to where the child is than the many diatonic tunes our 'methods' masters' publish by the endless series. My thesis supports, rather than supplants, the use of folk-song material, insisting, however, that we use the raw, unedited form untouched by the diatonic ditty writers who squeeze good folk tunes into the major scale. Take, for example, that wonderful Scotch ballad *Henry Martin* as sung by Burl Ives and accurately notated in the Kolb *Treasury of Folk Songs*. The section—'and they did cast lots'—falls into a pure Dorian mode in exactly the same way that Aaron Copland harmonizes the fiddle tune in the *Hoedown* from his ballet *Rodeo*.

"Children's experimentation in the unusual or irregular cannot be treated as a phase which precedes the study of the elements of diatonic music. The children's experiments *must constitute* the study. It is very easy for a teacher to smile approval only on the child's experiments which exactly fit the first-grade music book and so the child learns to reject his honest musical expressions and substitute those which might have been honest in the seventeenth century. Small wonder that so few show talent. The less talented ones are the ones that merely refuse to graft seventeenth-century ears on to a head that sees and imitates trains, airplanes, and fathers who play be-bop and Bartok. I certainly do not want to give the impression that I would force the child to fit my contemporary music mode instead of the classical mode, but I do strongly suggest that the experiences we bring to children should be of all kinds and should also contain contemporary material."

RESEARCH. Strangely enough we have practically no research in the musical significance of children's sound-making. We have always been too busy trying to teach children the music we know to pay serious attention to what they can do. The outstanding piece of investigation in this field—and it warrants careful study by the teacher—is that done by the Pillsbury Foundation[2] with very young children. Their studies in pamphlet form supplemented by the recordings of children's voices are recommended in increasing the listener's sensitivity.

Earlier in this chapter we suggested that we consciously listen to children's voices in a group. Let's turn the tables and listen to ourselves while we are waiting for a faculty or a parents' meeting to begin. The writer has become especially sensitive to college class sounds and can almost predict by the high pitch of voices a test or examination coming up next period. Usually the register of voices is one or two tones higher than on an average day when it is likely to hover around A flat. Sometimes it is fun to catch the "key" of the group as its members are talking with each other and "easily" play into it a selection on the piano or sing a song in the same key. Try it, and see what happens!

GROUP EXPERIMENTATION IN SOUND. We hope by this time the reader will be ready for what we have been working up to all the time and that is—eagerness to jump in and make sounds herself. Sometimes all a group needs is half a chance to open

[2] Pillsbury Foundation Studies. Phonograph Recordings of Spontaneous Music. Address: P.O. Box 1109, Santa Barbara, California.

up and let go with long repressed sounds as a mature music professor did recently when he gave vent to a shattering machine gun which he later confessed he had been itching to do for years. Again it may be necessary to turn out the lights or pull down the shades, for it is truly amazing what people can do when they feel that no one can see them. If it is still hard to get started, suggest that members of the group recall and reproduce children's sounds that tend to irritate teachers. Here we are almost certain to get a minor third chant with such words as "He is a sissy!" and usually it is as compelling with grown-ups as it is with children, i.e., everyone gets on the bandwagon with such momentum that one wonders if it will ever stop. Just for fun, try letting it go on until it wears down (perhaps after such an experience the chanters will have a little more sympathy with youngsters who do the same). When it dies down, pick it up again and experiment with it in ways as the following:

Divide the group in half. Let the first half start the chant and get well established with the rhythm. Have the other half *listen* and *listen* and then each one as an individual *feel* his way into what is going on and relate to it. Some may fall into the same pattern but others are sure to complement or supplement it or even come against it as in counterpoint. Out of the variety of responses—*and not until they have had some satisfaction in enjoying what they are doing*—we may choose one response and ask the group to listen to it for a moment. Then pair this off with one individual who is using the original chant and all listen. One might then build two groups—one around the original and one around the contrasting one. By this time all kinds of leads will present themselves as variations for use. It is hard to describe this kind of sound experimentation, for the outcome is always unpredictable—that's why it is such fun.

Its success depends on the extent to which the leader of the group has a quick ear for the unusual and is *willing to take a chance* with it.

What the leader is really doing is looking to individuals in the group for leadership, her job being that of a chairman who is seeking to extend the group experiences through many individual contributions. Her reasons for choosing one lead rather than another are varied. A very quiet member of a college class was interested in one of these sessions but never "let go" in the way the others did. Without knowing it, however, she was tapping out the rhythm of the sound play on her notebook. "Let's take her lead," said the teacher. The group listened and then used this student's simple quiet rhythm as a "theme." From this small beginning the group experimentation developed to the place where not only sound but also movement was used, this particular student leaving her seat and her original tapping and using her body in moving around the room in harmony with the group play.

Again the leader may recognize a significant musical lead in the sounds offered by the group and use this for a different purpose, such as helping the group be aware of the fact that they are having an experience in harmony or dynamics. This is really dealing directly with the raw materials of music, isn't it, without being handicapped by the lack of technical knowledge. In this way we are enriching our understanding of music through our inventions in pure sound. We started out with a minor third chant, but you see that we have lost it along the way by utilizing the inevitable variations and inventions supplied by individuals. Is not this matter of recognition of individual contributions perhaps as important as learning about music? Need we point out the implications here for working with youngsters? Would it frequently be the better part of wisdom to accept that annoying little drumming on the back row motivated probably by an unconscious need for release from tension or boredom, or probably a neat little plan to irritate teacher—accept it as a sign that the group would benefit by a few moments of relaxation? Wouldn't that class be surprised if teacher joined in the same rhythm and gave her sanction and even perhaps used her own initiative in helping everyone have a good time? When children realize that a teacher welcomes occasional sorties in the use of sound and rhythm that teacher will never need worry that she will not know how to proceed, for children will have many suggestions of what to do. Perhaps the group may develop sounds and rhythm that call for additional experiences such as songs or use of instruments or movement to be combined with the original.

Another interesting experiment in a class of grown-ups was suggested by a music student. Choose three or four people who speak different languages. Ask them to stand together and each speak—all at the same time—in his own language. They can say anything they want, tell a short story, or relate an experience. Ask the listening group to close their eyes and listen to the sounds of voices—differences in pitch, inflections, quality, pace. In a short time even though there are many variations, one will sense a kind of "sound" relatedness. This can also be done by using people who speak the same language but whose voices vary, or try having a group count together or say the alphabet over and over, letting come what may (that is the trick here; you must not plan ahead).

Another experience that groups enjoy is a more highly organized one. Divide the group into four sections and give each one the time value of a quarter note. Have the members of each section get together and decide how they will use this time and all agree to do the same thing. Then the leader claps out or plays a phrase of four measures in 4/4 time in order to get a group feeling for this rhythm. At a signal, group one takes the first count, group two the second, etc., each using only the time of one count. Since no group knows ahead what the other plans to do, this is full of surprises and fun. After a few rounds of this, folks become inventive and think up all kinds of stunts from absolute quiet to jumping up and giving a shout. There are many variations in the ways this can be handled, such as using different rhythms and giving a group an entire measure or a phrase. Older youngsters love this, too!

GROUP EXPERIENCES IN MOVEMENT. No group can experiment long with sound without becoming involved in some kind of movement even if it is only the tapping of feet or an almost imperceptible movement of the body. The two just naturally go together. Nor does it matter where we start, but frequently grown-ups feel more comfortable in beginning with sound experimentation. Once the group gets warmed up and a few "adventurers" start using movement, the leader, rather than taking a "sound" lead, may choose a movement and ask the group to follow. Or the suggestion may be given that everyone walk around the room (without music). No two people really walk alike. Some will swing their arms, some have a spirited quick walk, some are lackadaisical, some will walk in different directions, some give the appearance of walking with their whole body rather than with their feet. The leader then may take his cue from anyone (it is unfortunate to start out with a fancy stepper). Suppose we take, for example, a person who is walking in many different directions and ask everyone to experiment spatially (children do a specially skillful job in this). Then take another lead, and so on, working in the ways we described in sound. Sometimes youngsters call this playing "copy cat," and since this term has fallen into disrepute, we must point out that in a very real sense we all learn from others and to some extent copy them. If every member of a group is a potential "cat" to be copied and each has something unique to offer, then the teacher in recognizing these contributions is really capitalizing on the contributions of all. Does it matter what we call it?

ACCOMPANIMENT. Shall we have accompaniment? Many times an accompaniment as stamping feet, clapping hands, use of voices, use of instruments such as drums or piano will add to the experience. It is, however, so easy for all of us to be dominated by music and to respond to it rather than working with movement as a creative medium in itself that we strongly suggest holding back on accompaniment until the group is thoroughly at home in using movement independently of music. Then, of course, accompaniment may be chosen which will best promote the enrichment of the particular experience.

GROUP EXPERIENCES WITH INSTRUMENTS. Since we are concerned with musical experimentation that does not depend on formal lessons, the usual percussion instruments lend themselves most profitably to group use. Teachers will enjoy making many of these and can construct a good sound-making instrument. Barrels, nail kegs, wooden pails, hollow logs plus good skin drum heads may be used. Heads can be obtained at music instrument stores and occasionally satisfactory seconds may be acquired. Soaked in water for several hours, they should then be stretched over the open end of the keg and secured temporarily by thumbtacks. After drying overnight, if the skin is tight enough so as to give a pleasant sound, fasten it permanently with upholstery tacks. Much labor and busy work have gone on from time to time in this matter of making instruments, the outcome being anything but musical. Avoid cute tricks that are supposed to look like instruments but which have no musical possibilities. Other percussion instruments are gourds, maracas, sound boxes, rattles, wooden temple bells, rhythm sticks, and the piano, which in group experimentation may be used as a percussion instrument by someone who does not know how to play it!

Get together as many instruments as possible, and let each member of the group get acquainted with them, each in her own way. After a period of finding out about the instruments the leader again takes his cue from individuals in the group. When there are not enough instruments to go around, the other members may contribute sounds of voices, movements, and clapping.

OTHER MUSIC EXPERIENCES FOR TEACHERS. Several years ago some pre-service students who could not play a piano organized a guitar group. Enthusiasm was so great that some of them took their guitars to their student teaching centers after two lessons! And no one was more interested in helping these guitar players learn than the children in their schools. A guitar or ukulele are fairly simple instruments to play and lend themselves to informal and effective use with children. Other teachers have found recorders of real help. One experienced teacher was given an accordion for Christmas and was so excited about it that she took it to school the first day after vacation. Her children's expectations provided all the motivation she needed to learn to play. She did not dare let them down! Learning to play the piano can be fun, too, provided the music teacher is willing to work creatively with her students.

The auto harp is another instrument that many have found

helpful. It is more limited than a guitar, but it also requires less skill. It is important to keep it tuned, and older children can get some good ear training in doing this. Children enjoy using the auto harp and usually are much quicker than grown-ups in developing an ear for the right chords.

DANCE EXPERIENCES FOR TEACHERS. In addition to the experimentation in movement referred to above, one of the most rewarding experiences for teachers is to attend dance concerts. The choreography in current musical plays is of much interest since the dance composer works in movement, the accompaniment usually being composed for the dance. Watch or rather feel the movement of these dancers, their use of the whole body, their use of space, of the floor. The observer recognizes many of these movements as being similar to those that children use in free play. Naturally children are unaware of what they are doing, while the dancer is not only aware of but also can control his highly developed skill. The roots, however, of the art of movement are to be found in the child's spontaneous and free use of his body. Nothing can take the place of dancing itself—square, folk, social, and contemporary dance—as long as one does not become evangelistic about a particular school or system.

Teachers, too, need many opportunities to sing together—not "third-grade" songs, for the chances are slim that these will interest them. A long time needs to be spent singing what is of genuine interest to them, and many of these songs will also be of interest to children. Teachers, just as children, do not like to be "taught" all of the time. A music consultant working with them will find many opportunities, however, to extend singing repertories in many different directions.

Working with teachers in a great variety of ways would

seem to be a most profitable way to use at least part of the time of a music consultant, for to the extent that she can help teachers to find themselves musically, to be comfortable musically, to be willing to learn with children, and to utilize their own unique resources, we shall have a school interested in music. No, not all children in such a school will have identical experiences, but they will grow musically. Exposure, moreover, to the same program is no guarantee that there is acceptance of this program. Do we not stand a better chance of educating children musically in a school where many kinds of music are accepted?

9

PHONOGRAPH RECORDS

CHILDREN have a never-ending desire to investigate, to find out and to learn about the things they feel are important for them to learn. This curiosity frequently gets them into difficulty, and it also makes many demands upon the ingenuity, resourcefulness and patience of grown-ups. Earlier in this book we have considered children's curiosities in the raw materials of music and dance, i.e., in sound and rhythm as well as their interests in music and ways of guiding these interests. Music encompasses such a tremendous field of possible experiences that no one person, family, or school can possibly meet the variety and amount for which many children are eagerly reaching out. Also adults have other things to do, and even though they might be musically very competent, people cannot possibly "turn on" these experiences every time a child is ready for them.

We should, therefore, welcome any additional ways in which children can pursue their musical interests without benefit of adults. Phonograph records together with radio have revolutionized us within the past few years into a musically literate people, and it is nothing short of phenomenal the extent to which records can contribute to the musical growth of children from the cradle on. Give a two-year-old a group of well-chosen records, a small player, and he is independent—and how important this feeling of independence is when one is young and there are so many limitations on what one wants to do. He may choose his own time, his own records and *especially his own pace,* and depending on the child and the record he chooses, we may just as well be prepared to have our concept of the attention span of a two-year-old challenged. Records, then, can give a child an opportunity to go ahead on his own momentum, and where this momentum will take him is many times unpredictable. He will upset our finely spun theories of what is just the right music for the three-year-old or for an eight-year-old. He refuses to be packaged in neat compartments. Many music records not intended for the juvenile trade find a responsive chord in a child's heart. Snatches of the classics, ballads, and popular and folk music that are favorites of the grown-ups or the teen-agers will filter into his ears, and the process of discarding or taking from them what he likes goes on from day to day. He may even go off the deep end for a while and we may deplore his taste and feel certain he is going to end up as the leader of a popular band, but if he grows up in a home and school where there are a large variety of good records, his chances of coming through with a pretty reliable taste are good.

VARIETY IN RECORDS. Think of what recordings can do in bringing variety in music to children—variety in instruments, variety in the type of music. Every child should be free to browse through record collections which are not intended just for children. The present use of unbreakable disks ought to make teachers and parents feel comfortable about encouraging this. The child may choose Spike Jones or he may choose a string quartette. A few years ago a five-year-old had her own special part of a Mozart quartette that she played over and over at home. She occasionally brought the record to school and soon discovered that she was able to pick out the theme on the piano. That little girl, Susan, is now twelve years old and recently together with a friend, Jean, borrowed a dozen jive records from a college friend. When asked what they did with these records, Jean answered, "Oh, every Tuesday afternoon Susan comes to my house, and we lock ourselves in my room and play jive. We just can't wait for Tuesdays. Poor Susan—she has nothing but Brahms, Beethoven, and Mozart at her house." Both these girls have a truly fine appreciation for music, and their experiences are so deeply rooted that I am certain no amount of side excursions will permanently upset their musical discrimination.

STORIES ON RECORDS. There are many exciting things happening in the field of recorded stories and dramatic readings. What a boon to the overworked mother and teacher on whom there are so many demands for "just one more story." Not that records should ever take the place either in home or school of the told or read story, but when a child can turn to a record and hear over and over again a well-told story, he has at his command a truly wonderful resource for education. In choosing story records for children, we should demand honesty of approach, directness, and a voice that is non-patronizing, also a voice that is free of cuteness and studio overtones. Nor do good stories need dressing up in the way of exaggerated sound effects to interest children. An excellent record illustrating the simple, direct approach is *But Muffin Can Hear* (YPR) for the nursery- and kindergarten-age child. The narration is intimate, unhurried, and natural. Among the many good records for the younger elementary age are *Lentil* (YPR), *Horton Hatches the Egg* (MGM), and *Many Moons* (Columbia). And for the older children we have *Sinbad the Sailor, Three Musketeers,* and *Peter Pan,* all produced by Columbia. The American Library Association has done some outstanding work in records. Here we have straight story telling without sound effects or music, and there is no question about their holding children's interest in such stories as *A Paul Bunyan Yarn* and *A Pecos Bill Tale*. In some sections of the country book mobiles which serve rural areas are equipped with a loudspeaker, and when they stop at a school, they broadcast a record which stimulates a great demand for this story in book form.

Not only music, then, but also great literature and fine story telling can be turned to by the child of his own volition, and here again he may break down our notions of what we think will interest him. A twelve-year-old was listening to a recording of *Treasure Island* (Columbia). Her six-year-old brother was apparently completely absorbed in his own play. At the end of the story, however, he asked his sister for an explanation of certain parts that he did not understand. This album is now one of his favorites. Certainly one would not be likely to suggest buying this record for a six-year-old, and yet here was an experience from which this youngster took his own measure. At the same time a great favorite of his is a story about a little dog which is intended for the preschool child.

LEARNING FROM RECORDS. The foregoing illustration should cause us to stop and do some serious thinking about the many assumptions we make concerning children's interests, especially in our school programs. This is not only confined to music, but that is the field we are discussing here. An effective teacher is one who finds out what a child already knows so that she may do a better job of helping him learn more. But when one has thirty youngsters in a classroom, this is not an easy matter. A skillful person, however, can work with children in such a way so that they can be independent and she can give them many choices and opportunities. In other words, a third-grade teacher can take away the "third-grade" ceiling as laid down by tradition, the music course of study, or her own limitations, and allow children to learn what they are ready to learn. Make no mistake about it, we cannot force certain music experiences into them if they do not have a receptive attitude. What the clever child learns from such an experience—if he is not interested in it—is a technique of avoidance while giving the appearance of listening. He is learning how to pretend he is listening when he is not. How can we decide for any one group of children just what music should be learned or "appreciated" in a given year without knowing something about their musical capacities and tastes? This is where free choice in the school's collection of records can pay untold dividends—the greater the variety of recordings to choose from, the luckier the child in that school.

If children in a nursery school can operate their record player individually and independently (and they can), most certainly older boys and girls can do the same. And yet this opportunity is frequently denied them not because they are not responsible enough to manage the player but because playing records disturbs other children at work or because the only player in the school is a handsome large console model either in the music room or in the assembly hall and is used only for total group listening. Schools need portable record players that can be easily moved from room to room. If the sound disturbs others (often it is the teacher who is most disturbed), children can be helped to keep the volume turned low or ear phones may be attached so that they may use this resource for learning. It is not the intention here to suggest that all of the children's record experiences should be on an individual or small group basis. Certainly, there are many times when teachers and children, too, will want an entire group to have an experience together. If the discussion has seemed weighted on the side of individual use, it is because this has been sadly neglected and also because it can yield so much. Perhaps, too, it is a reaction against the "music appreciation" period via phonograph where emphasis is placed on identification of selection played, followed by a music test where the ability to name the piece and composer determine the pupil's musical rating. If test we must, why can we not have a test built on interest and pleasant associations?

DOCUMENTARY RECORDS. More and more companies are bringing out records relating to dramatic events in history such as Columbia's *Hear It Now,* Mike-ing History's *The Declaration of Independence,* which a twelve-year-old said sounded just like a report from the United Nations, and the Enrichment records based on the Landmark series of books on such subjects as the *Landing of the Pilgrims.* All of this material offers tremendous opportunities for pursuit of individual interests and independent study.

SKILLS AND PARTICIPATION RECORDS. There are also other types of factual material where there have been a number of trial records in teaching subject matter skills and still others that use a workbook or "how-to-teach" approach. They are mechanical and dull and deny everything we know about how learning goes on. There has also been a wave of "participation" records, the intention being to evoke response from the child in terms of physical activity—a worthy aim provided we remember that children participate in many different ways—at times even by being quiet. The trouble is, however, that when a writer aims at evoking activity he usually comes out with a contrived story that has no real point and precious little literary quality. What has just been said is not to be interpreted as saying that children should not be active in relation to records. They certainly should be if the story or music impels them to be, but let us work harder on producing good material and less on pushing children around.

STORY RECORD BOOKS. One of the most interesting developments in records is the story-book or record-reader album. In this the child can follow the story in the book while the record plays. The child who cannot read can follow the pictures while the one who likes to read or who is learning to read can follow the print, and how can we tell just when the non-reader begins to pick up a word here and there? Some teachers in the primary grades have been using some of these albums and have found them very helpful. Again it means that a child can be independent and in following the book he can read for himself. Not that we are suggesting that this is a system for teaching reading. No two children learn to read in the same way, and they also learn to read in many different ways. Many children, however, react most favorably to these albums. On the whole, the stories are good, the print is easy to read, the format is pleasing, and the pictures are attractive. Some favorites are Victor's *Little Engine That Could,* the upside-down books of *Winnie the Pooh and Eyore* and *Winnie the Pooh and Tigger,* MGM's *Tom and Jerry,* Capitol's Bozo series, the best of which are *Bozo at the Circus* and *Bozo on the Farm.* Parents and teachers should encourage record companies to produce more of this material, for there are many excellent stories that lend themselves well to this medium.

MUSIC RECORDS. When we consider the varied development in the field of children's records we find that those dealing with straight music have received too little attention. As was mentioned before, children absorb much from music intended for older people, and that is good. Some limitations, however, present themselves in that these records are not usually easily available to the younger children and also many of them are long compositions. Victor has a basic record library for elementary schools, a number of the records being made up of short excerpts of well-known music. Unfortunately, much of this material is not available on single disks, i.e., the entire volume has to be purchased. Also the organization of these records tends to define the use, although this does not seem to have been intended by the editors. If the school has these volumes, it is the responsibility of the teacher to familiarize herself with all the records and not to limit the musical experiences in terms of primary- or upper-grade classification.

A recent reissue of *Instruments of the Orchestra* (Victor), recorded some years ago in England under the direction of Sir Malcolm Sargent, is of interest. In this music each instrument is heard accompanied by the piano, the music is interesting in itself, and the plan is soundly conceived musically. In spite of the slightly scratchy surface characteristic of all former shellac records, the musical compensations are great. For older children Benjamin Britten's *The Young Person's Guide to the Orchestra* (Columbia) is unequaled. Musically important, too, are the "operettas" such as *The Emperor's New Clothes* (YPR) and *Sleeping Beauty* (CRG).

Recommended also are some records of music produced by children's record companies such as YPR's *Rondo for Bassoon* and *The Licorice Stick,* Mercury-Childcraft's *Great Music for Young Folks,* and others. Approach, however, with a critical ear the music records in which instruments are personified in order to teach the child. Children can and do take their music straight and personification as a teaching method harks back to the days of a now discredited psychology of learning. It not only confuses the child, but also it indicates slight respect for his ability to react directly to the art of music.

FOLK MUSIC. Children respond eagerly to folk music, and here we have a great deal of source material. The largest collection is to be found in the Library of Congress. This music has been recorded on the field and is authentic. It is not as acoustically smooth as the commercial recordings, but older boys and girls who are especially interested in studying the folk culture of different sections of our country will find it most rewarding. Folkways has given us some excellent records of the music of other countries and other cultures. Both teacher and children grow in exploring this music. Nor should we neglect to mention some of our current folk singers such as Burl Ives in *The Wayfaring Stranger* (Columbia), Josef Marais in *Songs of the Veld* (Decca), and Tom Glazer, who has recorded so many songs for YPR.

SOUNDS ON RECORDS. There are times when children are particularly interested in "sound" records either for the fun of just listening or for use in dramatic play. Every imaginable sound has been recorded and one can listen to everything from thunderstorms and railroad trains to crickets or tropical forest sounds. Also there are authentic birdcalls in *African Birds* by the American Museum of Natural History in New York and Comstock's *American Bird Album.*

SOURCES OF RECORDS. In discussing records we have indicated from time to time the names of the companies which produce them. Most of these records may be purchased through your local record store. An adequate record library either in one's home or in school is certainly to be desired, but there are other ways to obtain records, too. In some communities the local libraries have both a listening and a lending service. Family libraries should not be overlooked either by the school. Naturally, responsibility is assumed for careful handling. When schools have a certain amount of money in their budgets for records, it is hoped that the deciding and purchasing will not be done for the children by the teachers ahead of time. A group of children together with their teacher can have an extremely valuable experience in listening to a variety of records and deciding which ones they should like to have permanently. Perhaps they will make a few unwise choices (in the teacher's estimation) from time to time, but that is part of learning.

USE OF RECORDS AND MACHINE. Especially when younger children use records, the school must be prepared for certain replacements and minor repair jobs. But this is a small price to pay for the musical education that goes on when children are able to use records individually and independently. Besides, children grow in responsibility for equipment to the extent to which we give them opportunity to use this equipment, and it is amazing how even the youngest respond to our trust in them in this respect. It is far less serious to have an occasional accident to a record or machine than to have children live in an environment where they feel adults do not have faith in them.

What kind of record player should we buy? Shall it be single-speed or three-speed? How much does one have to pay for a satisfactory machine? It is not easy to answer these questions, for there is such rapid development in this field that today's answers may be outdated in no time at all. *At the present time* the 78 rpm (revolutions per minute) is generally used in nursery, kindergarten, and primary grades since the majority of children's records are still being made on this speed. The 45-rpm player is excellent, but it is limited to 45-rpm records. A fairly adequate player may be had for $25 to $30, keeping in mind that it is important to have a light-weight pickup, a reasonable-sized speaker, and sound but not fancy construction. Three-speed portables cost from $50 to $100 and require more careful handling than the single speed, but by the time children are interested in long-playing records they are able to operate the machine. The "permanent" needle also needs to be replaced from time to time. When we notice a rattle or raspiness in the record, especially near the center, the chances are that it is the needle and not the record that is at fault.

Where should the player be placed? Where children can watch the disk go round and round. For the younger children a low table or the floor is suitable, and older youngsters can make their own arrangements. It is hard to understand, but there seems to be something almost hypnotic in this desire to watch the turntable. Perhaps the rhythm of the movement relaxes children and helps them to listen. At any rate, accept the fact, and arrange for them to be close to this experience both in school and at home.

The records listed on pages 145-149 are only a few of the great number available. The plan here is to suggest records that meet a wide variety of interests rather than choosing only the best. Because of the lack of space, many excellent records, especially in music, have been omitted and also the ones mentioned in the discussion in this chapter have not been listed again. Any classification of records *must* be used with flexibility. This is especially true in music where so much depends on individual taste and experience.

RECORDS

A—Allegro	D—Decca	MGM—Metro Goldwyn Mayer
BEL—Belda	FW—Folkways	V—RCA Victor
BOR—Bornand	H—Haydn Society	YPR—Young People's Records
CAP—Capitol	L—London	
CRG—Children's Record Guild	MER—Mercury	
COL—Columbia	MC—Mercury Childcraft	

MUSIC

Records generally produced for adults but enjoyed by many children

America's Favorite Marches (Cities Service Band)	V
Coppelia Ballet Suite, Delibes (orchestra)	V
Entrance of Little Fauns, Pierne; *Espara-Waltz,* Waldteufel (orchestra)	COL
Folk Dance Records	V
Folk Music of Haiti (native), 4–10″	FW
Folk Songs of Brazil, Bidu Sayao	COL
Gayne Ballet Suites, Khachaturian (orchestra), 3–12″	COL
Grand Canyon Suite, Grofe	V
Great Music for Young Folks	MC
Hansel and Gretel (opera), 12–12″. Complete opera recorded by the Metropolitan Opera Company	COL
Haydn's Toy Symphony	V
Historical America in Song, with Burl Ives, 6 albums (Encyclopædia Britannica)	

Hungarian Dances Nos. 5 and 6, Brahms gypsy melodies (Boston "Pops" Orchestra) V
Invitation to the Dance, Weber (orchestra) COL
Let's Listen to Haydn, 10″ LP (excellent) H
Marche Militaire, Schubert V
Music Box, Liadof V
Music of the Sioux and Navajo, 4–10″ FW
Nutcracker Suite, Tchaikovsky V
Peer Gynt Suite, Grieg V
Rodeo, Aaron Copland. Four dance episodes (orchestra), 3–12″ V
Rondino on a Theme by Beethoven, Kreisler; *Orpheus Melody,* Gluck (violin and piano) COL
Rosamunde, Schubert (orchestra) COL
Songs of Many Lands, Josef Marais and Miranda, 4–10″ D
Sweet and Low, Music box record BOR
Symphony 5½, Don Gillis, 10″ LP. Composer has a hilarious time with sound L
The Wayfaring Stranger, Burl Ives COL
Waltzes, Brahms (2 pianos) MER
William Tell Overture, Rossini V

Records produced for children, some combining story and music with comments

A-hunting We Will Go. Old hunting songs YPR
Animal Fair, Burl Ives, 2–10″. Funny songs made especially for children COL
Bozo's Circus Band, 10″ LP CAP
The Clock That Went Backwards. Music back to primitive time CRG
Come to the Fair. Spirited singing YPR
Concerto for Toys and Instruments (excellent) YPR

Folk Songs of Other Lands. Songs in English, French and German	MC
Folk Songs of Our Land	MC
Golliwog's Cakewalk, Debussy; *Ecossaises,* Chopin (piano)	YPR
The Lonesome House	CRG
Interesting experiment in creative use of sound	
The Neighbor's Band	YPR
Robin Hood. Spirited musical play, 2–10″	YPR
Rondo for Bassoon	YPR
Songs for Sleepy Heads	MC
Songs of Our Patriots	MC
Square Dance Party	CAP
Walk in the Forest (excellent for very young child)	YPR

MUSIC AND STORIES

(The following age classifications are intended to be used *only as a guide.* There is much overlapping, and also individual differences play an important part in choice of records.)

Younger child (2 to 6 years of age)

Bells of Calais, "Frère Jacques"	YPR
The Elephant and the Flea	A
Fog Boat Story	CRG
Grandfather's Farm	CRG
Hansel and Gretel	MC
Little Brass Band	YPR
The Little Gingerbread Man	MGM
The Men Who Come to Our House	YPR
Mother Goose Parade. Sensitive use of music and sound	MGM
Mother Goose Series, 6 records	MC

The Owl and the Pussy Cat A
Runaway Sheep. Delightful use of real shepherd's pipe YPR
Singing Games MGM
The Three Little Pigs MGM
Train to the Farm. Songs about animals CRG
Tunes for Wee Folks MC
Whoa, Little Horse YPR

Older child (5 to 12 years of age)

Alice in Wonderland, 6–12" V
The Bear That Wasn't, 4–10" MGM
By Rocket to the Moon YPR
The Concertina That Crossed the Country YPR
Cowboys and Indians A
Destination Moon CAP
Gerald McBoing-Boing by Dr. Seuss CAP
Riotous "tongue in the cheek" story
Hansel and Gretel. Humperdinck classic enacted by Basil Rathbone as the narrator COL
I've Been Working on the Railroad YPR
Lewis Carroll: Alice in Wonderland, 4–12" COL
Little Pedro. Latin American game songs in Spanish and English CRG
The Little Fiddle. Riotous fun with Danny Kaye D
The Lonesome Octopus. Talking comics BEL
The Man Who Invented Music, 1–12" LP. Delightful tall tale L
Peter and the Wolf V
Ship Ahoy. Sea chanteys CRG
There Were Three Indians. Introduction to history MGM
Tubby the Tuba, Danny Kaye D
The Twelve Days of Christmas YPR

The Underground Train YPR
Who Built America. American history through folk songs, 2–12″ FW

RECORD STORY-BOOK ALBUMS

(Story, pictures, records)

Bugs Bunny in Storyland CAP
Bugs Bunny and the Tortoise CAP
The Grasshopper and the Ants CAP
Little Black Sambo's Jungle Band V
Mr. I. Magination Meets Rip Van Winkle. Music score and pictures COL
Pinocchio V
Tom and Jerry MGM

SUGGESTED READING FOR PARENTS AND TEACHERS

Marion Bauer and Ethel Peyser. *How Music Grew.* Putnam
——*Music Through the Ages.* Putnam
Helen Christianson (compiler). *Music and the Young Child.* Bulletin of the Association for Childhood Education, 1201 Sixteenth St., N. W., Washington, D. C.
John Dewey. *Art as Experience.* Minton, Balch
Angela Diller. *Keyboard Music Study,* Books I and II. Schirmer
Charlotte G. Garrison and Emma Dickson Sheehy. *At Home with Children.* Henry Holt
Howard D. McKinney and W. R. Anderson. *Discovering Music.* American Book Company
Douglas Moore. *Listening to Music.* Norton
James L. Mursell. *The Psychology of Music.* Norton
——*Education for Musical Growth.* Ginn
——*Music and the Classroom Teacher.* Silver Burdett
Beatrice Perham. *Music in the New School* (rev. ed.). Kjos Music Co.
M. Emett Wilson. *How to Help Your Child with Music.* Schumann

COMPOSER BIOGRAPHIES WRITTEN FOR YOUNG PEOPLE

Elliott Arnold. *Finlandia: the Story of Sibelius.* Henry Holt (rev. ed.)

Gladys Burch. *Richard Wagner: Who Followed a Star.* Henry Holt (rev. ed.)

David Ewen. *Haydn.* Henry Holt

—— *Tales from the Vienna Woods: the Story of Johann Strauss.* Henry Holt

Madeleine Goss. *Beethoven: Master Musician.* Henry Holt (rev. ed.)

—— *Deep-Flowing Brook: the Story of Johann Sebastian Bach.* Henry Holt (rev. ed.)

—— *Unfinished Symphony: the Story of Franz Schubert.* Henry Holt (rev. ed.)

Madeleine Goss and Robert Haven Schauffler. *Brahms: the Master.* Henry Holt

Dena Humphreys. *On Wings of Song: the Story of Mendelssohn.* Henry Holt

Ann Lingg. *Mozart.* Henry Holt

Claire Lee Purdy. *He Heard America Sing: the Story of Stephen Foster.* Messner

—— *Song of the North: the Story of Edvard Grieg.* Messner

—— *Stormy Victory: the Story of Tchaikovsky.* Messner

Opal Wheeler and Sybil Deucher. *Edward MacDowell and His Cabin in the Pines.* E. P. Dutton